STO

ACPL ITEM

DISCARDED

P9-BHR-666

7-1-63

THE
DYNAMICS OF
CHURCH
GROWTH

THE
DYNAMICS OF
CHURCH
GROWTH

J. Waskom Pickett

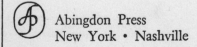
Abingdon Press
New York • Nashville

THE DYNAMICS OF CHURCH GROWTH

Copyright © 1963 by Abingdon Press

All rights in this book are reserved.
No part of the book may be reproduced in any
manner whatsoever without written permission of
the publishers except brief quotations embodied in
critical articles or reviews. For information address
Abingdon Press, Nashville 2, Tennessee.

Library of Congress Catalog Card Number: 63-7767

Scripture quotations unless otherwise noted are from the
Revised Standard Version of the Bible, copyrighted 1946
and 1952 by the Division of Christian Education, National
Council of the Churches, and are used by permission.

SET UP, PRINTED, AND BOUND BY THE
PARTHENON PRESS, AT NASHVILLE,
TENNESSEE, UNITED STATES OF AMERICA

1226925

To the parents and parents-in-law,
wife, children and children-in-law,
and grandchildren
who have provided massive social support
for my Christian faith and purpose

FOREWORD

I write this foreword to Bishop Pickett's book with great satisfaction. He is known to the whole church in India primarily as an evangelist who spent himself in the task of making Jesus Christ known, accepted, and obeyed. His leadership in the mass-movement work of the Indian church and his interpretation of it has been invaluable.

In this book he brings to bear on the subject of church expansion his deep commitment, extensive experience, and power of presentation. The classic book on the subject with which Bishop Pickett deals is that of Donald McGavran entitled *Bridges of God*. To this book, Bishop Pickett adds very useful emphasis. His is a fresh and most encouraging statement of the urgency and possibility of church expansion. He writes out of a vast missionary and church experience.

I commend this book in the hope it will receive the attention it deserves and will promote the cause for which it is intended.

D. T. NILES
Jaffna, Ceylon

INTRODUCTION

Each year Northwest Christian College through its Institute of Church Growth presents an outstanding missionary thinker, speaking on the continuing and central purpose of missions—planting and multiplying Christian churches throughout the world. These Annual Lectures are published in our "Church Growth Series."

The first lecturer, speaking in the fall of 1961 on "The Dynamics of Church Growth," was J. Waskom Pickett—an extraordinarily able churchman. A missionary since 1910, a bishop of The Methodist Church in Southern Asia since 1936, for many years a member of the inner circle in the National Christian Council of India, since 1957 a professor of missions at Boston University, and a consultant to his board visiting many lands to study the expanding Church, he knows the problems and achievements of the younger Churches. Author of *Christian Mass Movements in India* and *Christ's Way to India's Heart* and coauthor of *Church Growth and Group Conversion*, his have been the pioneer appraisals of the church-growth situation.

The Dynamics of Church Growth bristles with new insights of vast importance and will have marked influence in missions for many years. Its optimistic thinking is welcome in the midst of today's uncertainty. The World Mission of the Church needs this message at this time. Among other things, it argues that but for the tremendous effort of Protestant missions, all Asia and Africa by now would have crumbled before Communism.

Bishop Pickett insists that service and evangelism must not be substituted for nor separated from each other. Both were evidenced in the earthly life of our Lord, and are essential for church growth. This emphasis is greatly needed in two quarters—where men preach the Word careless as to whether love is shown, and where Christians show love careless as to whether men are brought to Christ or churches multiplied.

Donald McGavran, Director
Institute of Church Growth
Eugene, Oregon

CONTENTS

9

CONTENTS

I

The Case for Rapid Growth

Admittedly there is in many areas much feeling against the rapid accession of new members to the church. It is fashionable to condemn popular movements in religion as hysterical, shallow, and destructive of spiritual values. But how much is that feeling due to understanding and objective appraisal? How much of it rests on pure impressionism and cannot be sustained by factual data?

My observations in many lands and careful scientific surveys in India and Pakistan have led me to the conclusion that natural, rapid community or group movements to Christian discipleship are more likely to produce a strong, healthy church than are cautiously controlled processes of slow growth. Generally speaking, slow growth indicates something wrong with the quality of life of the church. It both reflects and produces churches that lack either the urge to make disciples or the triumphant faith necessary to translate such urge into effective endeavor. Is it not reasonable to suppose that a church in which the Holy Spirit is at work in pentecostal power would experience the rapid growth that took place in Jerusalem after Pentecost?

There is abundant evidence on every continent that people

11

are helped in coming to Christian faith and purpose and in living therein when friends, relatives, and associates share the experience with them and are hindered when they come alone breaking with loved ones and neighbors. Social support in living the good life is a necessity for all of us, and social dislocation for anyone anywhere at any time is a tragedy. Jesus said that the kingdom of God is like leaven. It spreads among people as leaven spreads in dough. To take the new convert away from his associates is like taking the leaven out of the dough. It is not good for him, his associates, or the church. It interferes with his growth in Christ, deprives his former associates of an influence they need for their soul's good, and retards the growth of the church. Every new convert is a potential evangelist and grows in grace as he spreads the evangel to others.

The early church, led directly by men trained by our Lord, grew rapidly. Following the first Pentecost, when Peter in public preaching fervently called for repentance and baptism for the remission of sins, about three thousand were added to the church. How much these new members had known of Jesus, his work and his teachings, before their response to Peter's sermon, we do not know. Some may have heard him preach and may have seen him heal the sick or even have been healed in mind and body by the touch of his hand or the power of his word. Some may even have been in the company that turned back and followed him no more after hearing him proclaim himself as "the bread which came down from heaven." In any case the test of discipleship when these three thousand joined the church seems to have been receiving the Word from the apostles, declaring their faith, and repenting of their sins; not the length of their association with the apostles, the thoroughness of their training, or demonstrative proof of their conversion. After they were baptized and admitted to church membership, the book of Acts tells us "they devoted themselves to the apostles' teaching and fellowship, to the breaking of bread and the prayers."

Postbaptismal instruction, fellowship with one another and with the earlier disciples, and united worship met the spiritual needs of those new church members and made them zealous and effective evangelists. In the Acts of the Apostles it is put thus: "Day by day attending the temple together and breaking bread in their homes, they partook of food with glad and generous hearts, praising God and having favor with all the people." And the church continued to grow rapidly. "The Lord added to their number day by day those who were being saved."

Clearly these early converts became one people. Many walls of separation must have been broken down in those days. Theirs was a wide-community movement. A force stronger than the differences which had kept these people apart—their provincial distinctions of speech and dress, their prejudices in the politics of state and temple, and their arguments about creed—brought them together in a comprehensive and enriching fellowship.

The favor with which the public viewed these developments in the life of the church was not shared by the priests of Israel or by the secular beneficiaries of the then prevailing *status quo*, the officers and servants of the alien government, or by the many who for varied reasons sought the favor of one group or the other of these oppressors. Peter, and presumably the other apostles, encouraged by the rapid growth of the church, fearlessly criticized the priests and the rulers and even publicly charged the people with guilt for consenting to the death of Jesus.

What a transformation had taken place in Peter since the day when he lacked courage to admit even to a servant girl that he had been with Jesus! The shrinking, timid Galilean fisherman had become, under the impact of the Resurrection and Pentecost and by the enrichment of apostolic service, a man of fearless courage. As he boldly denounced their wickedness he proclaimed the love of God and promised forgiveness. "I know that you acted in ignorance, as did also your rulers. . . . Repent therefore, and turn again, that your sins may be blotted out, that times of refreshing may come from the presence of the Lord." Here we see the most wonderful of the works of Jesus: an average sort of man—mediocre, weak, and sinful—remade into an apostle combining within himself the character and the functions of the fearless prophet and the minister of reconciliation. Matthew, reporting another of the wondrous works of Jesus, wrote: "The dumb man spoke; and the crowds marveled." Possibly many of those who were converted first marveled at the transformation they saw in Peter and then recognized it as evidence of the truth of what he preached.

While the common people continued to respond with penitence and faith, the priests and the captain of the temple and the Sadducees came and arrested Peter and John. The Sadducees were angry because the apostles were teaching that Jesus had risen from the dead, and so joined the exploiting priests and the agents of Roman colonialism in this act of oppression. How often, since then, has a like combination of the orthodox priest, the religious skeptic, and the political tyrant been formed to destroy or control the church! But this unnatural alliance could not, at least did not, stop the growth of the church. Rather it turned out like Paul's later imprisonment in Rome "for the furtherance of the gospel." Many more believed the word of the apostles and became evangelists, spreading the good news. The man who wrote the biblical account of this revival, Luke, says: "The number of the men came to about five thousand." Despite his Christian training and experience he was so much a man of his time that he did not report the number of women and children. Perhaps five thousand men would indicate a community of twenty thousand persons.

In this period of quick growth some were baptized who later fell away. Ananias and his wife, Sapphira, were received into the church and coveted recognition as fervent, self-sacrificing members. They tried to deceive other members about the measure of their devotion. But that cannot be charged against rapid growth, for slow growth and man-made tests of fitness for membership have never precluded misbehavior by an occasional church member. Even the selective process and thorough training followed by our Lord in choosing and preparing officers of the church did not prevent falling away. The twelve were selected in ones and twos and most carefully trained for three years. They witnessed the mighty works of Jesus, they heard the even mightier words of his public preaching and teaching and of his intimate conversations with them as a group and, doubtless, with each of them in private. Yet Judas betrayed him, Peter denied him, and James and John and all the others forsook him before he went to the cross.

On theological, sociological, and psychological grounds the case for rapid growth is very strong.

Let us consider the theological grounds first. Christian faith predicates powerful and persistent love by God for every human being. All people are God's children. The poet puts this clear teaching of Jesus into song:

> That He who made all nations is not willing
> One soul should perish, lost in shades of night.

Matthew quotes our Lord as instructing the surviving eleven, as they greet and worship him with revived faith atop a mountain in Galilee after the Resurrection, to "make disciples of all nations," and as fortifying them with the declaration, "All authority in heaven and on earth has been given to me," and with the blessed assurance, "Lo, I am with you always, to the close of the age." Before these unfaithful men met the risen Lord and heard him speak these majestic words of announcement, command, and promise, they were discouraged, depressed, and unbelieving. But as they responded to him their doubts and fears left them. As they began telling others what they knew of Jesus that knowledge became more precious and convincing to them. Especially after Pentecost their joyful consciousness of the presence of their Lord and their complete acceptance of the responsibility he had given them made them more than conquerors. It is not recorded that any one of the eleven ever again doubted or failed him.

What Jesus had preached and instructed his disciples to preach was then, is now, and forever will be relevant to every man, woman, and child in every part of God's world. It cannot be withheld from any nation or person without sin. So long as the church gave itself unreservedly to making disciples it prospered, despite opposition and persecution. And when it became disobedient and negligent, its own life and health declined.

16

After a missionary had preached the gospel at Nairobi, Kenya, to an audience of several hundred people from India and had closed with the expressed hope that many in the audience would be converted, a leader of the group arose and protested because the preacher had not expressed hope for the conversion of all present. "Which ones does God not love?" he asked. The missionary felt condemned. To plan for slow growth of the church, to prefer it to rapid growth, such as followed Pentecost, and to proclaim slow growth as the will of God is open to the gravest theological objections and cannot be reconciled with the central affirmation that Jesus made about God.

The sociological case for rapid growth is likewise compelling. No one lives to himself alone. Not one of us can be a spiritual Robinson Crusoe. No human personality is complete within itself. We are parts of one another. All are dependent on others for support in living a life acceptable to God. Jesus trained the disciples together, not separately. They had a three-year course in community living as a part of their preparation for the ministry of the Word and the Sacraments. In their final commissioning they were told to make disciples of nations, not of a few people in every nation, as some seem to think the Lord meant to say, or should have said.

The apostles and those associated with them in the small pre-Pentecost fellowship were not afraid of rapid growth. They did not think it necessary to screen all would-be disciples. It was sufficient to ask candidates for baptism and church membership to repent of their sins and believe on the Lord Jesus Christ. That call, as part of a ministry which included confident preaching of the gospel, healing of the sick, hospitality, community oneness, and fellowship in group prayer, produced massive character

17

transformation and personality enrichment. For that result, rapid growth was not just desirable; it was essential. For meeting the complicated needs of today's confused world, such growth is not optional but mandatory. Rarely have group spiritual needs been so apparent, and never have group sins more rigidly controlled or more seriously threatened individuals than now. Never has there been more urgent need for group therapy.

As unbelief persisted among the twelve during their training, necessitating frequent reproof by the Lord, so unbelief persists in the church today. As it made the twelve unstable so it makes multitudes unstable now. People who should be ministering to others have to be ministered unto. The conversion of nations which have long suffered from the tyrannies of paganism, superstition, priestcraft, and "strong-man" rule is delayed by the fickleness and folly of professed Christians who are not faithful. But as the doubts and fears and hesitations of early disciples finally disappeared and they gave all-embracing personal and group obedience to the missionary mandate of their risen Lord, so at many places in the church of today, groups of disciples are experiencing the therapy of revival and rapid growth through zealous corporate obedience.

Without the experience of Pentecost and the triumphant spiritual and numerical growth to which it led directly, the church surely could not have survived the sustained effort of imperial Rome and her allies for its destruction. And without the outreach that brought hundreds of thousands to Christian conviction and dedicated discipleship, the church could never have accumulated its matchless store of inspiring records of heroes, saints, and martyrs.

Our Lord did everything possible to implant in the minds of

his disciples the expectation of rapid growth. They saw how he healed the sick and preached to throngs, how he sought to reach masses by meeting the needs of individuals, how he never lost sight of the individual in the crowd or of the crowd around the individual. When what he had done for a few brought multitudes to him, he exhorted his disciples to recognize the needs of those throngs and to accept responsibility to do something under God for them. "Pray therefore the Lord of the harvest to send out laborers." After they had prayed, presumably, he appointed them to be the laborers and instructed them to do exactly what he had been doing. They were to preach the gospel, "heal the sick, raise the dead, cleanse the lepers, and cast out demons."

Leaders of India's oppressed castes, now often called Harijans, and of Africa's hitherto underprivileged tribes have extolled Christian missions for heroic service to their people but have lamented the slow pace of church growth. An associate of the late Dr. Ambedkar, first Law Member in Nehru's cabinet, said: "I am a Chamar [leather-worker]. There are millions of us. We have been badly abused in Hinduism, starved, insulted, and despised. We are ignorant, crude, cruel, and dirty. We live in hovels. But we must change. Our children must have a different sort of life. You Christians have what we need, the right kind of religion. It works now for a few of our people. Some who have come to know Christ have proved that Chamars can be as good and as smart as any people, but you are too slow. We cannot wait. By your program it would take generations for all our people to be rescued. We will have to find a quicker way."

In Africa, too, such thinking is often encountered. A Christian teacher in Southern Rhodesia said: "I get impatient with the

19

church. The missionaries talk about making us church members better Christians, before we start new churches. In the meantime more beer halls are opened every year and more simple Africans learn evil Western ways. It takes only a few days for a villager to be corrupted by city ways, but months for him to find acceptance as a Christian. The wicked quickly make him one of themselves, while the pastors keep him waiting for months before they make him one of us. They must test him and prove him before they adopt him. If they would adopt him at once and treat him as a son in Christ, he'd respond much more quickly."

Both in India and in Africa, there are many Christian men and women who could be effective unpaid evangelists and lay helpers to the pastors. With their help the rate of church growth could be significantly increased. Islam is spreading rapidly in Africa, without professional direction. But in many Christian churches and missions the professional controls the situation completely, and the unpaid evangelist's efforts are not encouraged. We need to see how Islam, without having a priesthood and without appointing missionaries, often triumphs over the Christian missionary effort. The same lesson can be learned even more effectively by a penitent perusal of the book of Acts.

A group in South India decided that their welfare and that of their children required that they become Christians. They pooled their knowledge and understanding and began holding worship services without the help of an ordained minister or even a layman appointed by his church to do such work. They met each day to pray, sing, and read the Bible. Then the pastors moved in on them and objected to anyone teaching or preaching until he was approved by the diocesan authorities. That kind of control allows only slow growth and is not compensated for by the better quality of leadership. It also encourages the charge of religious imperialism. When the ordained minister claims exclusive right to proclaim the evangel to the unconverted it is almost inevitable that he will be accused of making proselytes rather than disciples. And the growth of the church is slowed down. The simplicity of the message of Jesus contrasts with the complex elaboration of denominational requirements regarding knowledge of church polity, ritual, and creedal emphases.

The chief obstacles to the conversion of large numbers of people are not sins for which they as individuals are wholly or chiefly responsible. They are sins of the group of which they are members or of the society in which they are enmeshed. A Brahman who was drawn to Jesus by what he read in the Bible and saw in the church, but who met terrific opposition from his family, caste associates, and neighbors, said: "It is so difficult for a Brahman to be converted and so easy for an Untouchable. I could wish I were one of those whom men despise. It would be so much easier for me to be saved." He saw the obstacles which Brahman society and the larger Hindu community had placed on his road to Christian discipleship. He did not realize how many obstacles that same Hindu community under the same Brahman leadership had piled up in the way of the Untouchables' approach to Christ. But perhaps he vaguely sensed the fact that Untouchables had found a way to move together into the Kingdom, preserving group life and providing needed social support for one another.

The privileged classes in Galilee and Judea did not acclaim Jesus and respond to him as did the common people, the weak, the poor, and the sick. Their privileged status was in itself an obstacle that kept Roman government officials and employees and army officers, and even private soldiers, and Jewish priests and their attendants and associates in the hierarchy from following Jesus. Their unenviable ordinariness made it less difficult for the Galilean fishermen to follow Jesus and to respond to his teachings.

Theological and sociological considerations coalesce to give added support to the case for rapid growth in some areas. Many oppressive social customs grow out of erroneous conjectures of men about God. The Iban in Sarawak who has killed a member of another tribe, cut off his head, and brought it to his longhouse residence has done what the religious conjectures of his ancestors assumed would please their tribal gods. Even cannibalism has been supported by mistaken ideas of what God wants or about the supreme God and the lesser gods. In one society with polytheistic beliefs it has been found difficult for individuals to protect themselves and members of their families against smallpox because of the widely established belief that smallpox is spread by a goddess who must be conciliated by community-wide processions singing her praises and making offerings to her. Christian converts have been forced by threats and beatings to join those processions. One group abandoned Christian discipleship through shame and a malfunctioning sense of guilt because they had participated, though under protest, in such a procession. During the Mau Mau terrorism in Kenya many Kikuyus accepted martyrdom rather than renounce their Christian faith or commit the crimes the terrorists demanded of them. But many others of that tribe were kept from Christ by the sins of hate and murder, organized and promoted against their will and over their protest as individuals by the group to which they belonged. It should be clear to disciples of Jesus that they must not ignore group sins by addressing their appeal for penitence and promise of pardon only to individuals. To do so is to condone group sin in all the dimensions of family, local community, corporate business, clan, caste, and nation. And those are the sins that now threaten unprecedented devastation everywhere.

A Brahman college student in North India, hearing the gospel preached for the first time, remarked to the preacher: "If one could believe what you have said about God's love for all people it would be a comforting doctrine. But I can't believe it! If you had said, 'God loves you Brahmans,' I would reply, 'Yes, see how well he treats us.' But when you say that he loves the Untouchables, I know you are wrong, for he shows them no love."

The preacher replied: "God did not make some Brahmans and others Untouchables. He made men. But some men made themselves Brahmans and others Untouchables. God continues to love the Brahmans despite their sin of making others of his children Untouchables."

Obviously people whose way of life and behavior have been determined by a non-Christian society of which they are a part need social help if they are to meet the behavior demands of Christian discipleship. If they break with their old society they only gain a desired measure of freedom from its control, but they lose social support where it is needed. If then they do not obtain social support from their new society they are in very grave danger.

Where a change of faith and allegiance takes place in groups so that the converts do not lose social adjustment, the church gains immensely. And relations with those on the outside are not so seriously impaired. Few things are so resented by group-

23

conscious people as are those actions that disrupt group life. And the Christian witness of a group which has been converted and has been protected against disruption and whose life has been enriched and uplifted is far more effective than is that of any loosely related aggregation of detached individuals.

In the Congo it is clear that the church has grown by spreading within the channels of tribal life. But the emphasis on individualism, imported from Europe and America, has so influenced African church leaders that they have hesitated to recognize and admit the fact even to themselves. "We pay no attention to a man's tribe. We call every man and every woman to penitence and faith without asking about his tribe." Thus spoke a prominent pastor at Elisabethville, but a factual study showed that nearly all his church members were brought to Christ by friends within their own tribe. And in almost every aspect of their lives they were influenced by their respective tribal origins. That pastor had slowed down the growth of the church and severely limited the impact of the gospel by refusing to recognize the facts of tribal life as real and meaningful.

Psychology adds heavy weight to the case for rapid church growth. We of the human family, whatever our race, nationality, or religion of origin, are subject to the same general laws of psychology. These laws operate in widely varying social and economic conditions. In one country after another evidence abounds that a growing church commends the gospel to onlookers as a static church does not. People brought up within one religion are rarely indifferent when, for the first time, they see another religion, but they are quite prone to form an unfavorable judgment on it. Unless they see proof of something attractive that they have not known in their old religion they quickly conclude that the new religion has nothing distinctive and especially good to offer them. Even if they see something that appeals to them personally, its influence upon them will be very limited if it seems to make little or no appeal to others within their group or their circle of associates. Those with whom they feel a community of interest, or to whose judgments they are prone to conform, may create for them a climate of rejection.

This influence of our fellows upon us as individuals is clearly recognized in business, politics, and entertainment. It is the basic fact upon which modern advertising rests. A new science of public relations has arisen with men especially trained in its use. Through the media of print, radio, television, and motion pictures this new science is being used to manipulate public opinion for economic, political, and military ends. The church by its very nature and by its Holy Cause is restrained in the use it can make of this science but it cannot ignore the facts upon which the science is founded. Enemies of the kingdom of God have too long been permitted to use this science without an adequate challenge by those who are called to defend the gospel.

In an area in India, where Christian missions had been at work only a few years, several hundred people of an underprivileged caste confessed faith in Christ and were baptized. They gave sufficient proof of their conversion to make the missionaries and Indian ministers who were in association with them confident that God was at work among them and that they were responding to him. Then thousands of people of the same social stratum called for Christian teaching with a view to baptism and church membership. Trained preachers able to enter sympathetically into the problems of these people and knowing their dialect were not available.

25

A few ministers were imported from another area two hundred miles distant. They were without successful experience in ministering to very poor and oppressed rural people. They pleaded for caution and warned against rapid action. The missionary sought advice but found no one who had ever dealt with such a situation as his. He therefore moved slowly and tried to "consolidate the position." But contrary to his expectations he found that those thousands who pleaded in vain for instruction, acceptance, and pastoral care soon lost interest and decided that they had been deluded in hoping for a new life in the church. Some turned hostile and began opposing the church. Not only this, but the few hundred upon whom the missionary and his colleagues had concentrated their attention lost much of their fervor. Years later the missionary declared: "If I could recover the opportunity of those early years I would not hesitate as I did then. I would trust God and those eager, seeking thousands. There would be a church of tens of thousands there now had I not been afraid, and I am compelled to believe as a result of my observations and studies since then, they would be on the average far better Christians than the hundreds to whom we restricted the gospel because of our timidity and lack of faith."

Surely the case for rapid growth is proved and the hesitations of the past should be abandoned. Where group movements are natural they should be welcomed with joy. The whole church should now accept its responsibility and begin a united and much more fervent effort to bring the nations to Christian faith and purpose. That is Christ's way to the heart of people everywhere—the Royal Road to the kingdom of God.

II

The Tragedy of Retarded Growth

The child whose physical or mental growth is retarded excites pity. He is pathetic. The case of the retarded church is even more tragic because it means the impoverishment and crippling, not of one individual only, but of masses of God's people—in families, communities, and nations.

All members are likely to suffer spiritually if the processes of growth in any church are interrupted. The oldest and most mature members need to know that God continues to work through the fellowship of which they are a part, so that the gospel is being confirmed afresh day by day. And the youngest and least mature members need assurance that others of their age and condition are acknowledging that Christ is Lord and Savior.

Whenever and wherever the church fails to witness effectively for Christ its growth is retarded. Loss of vitality and character in church members, adverse verdicts of children on the religion of their parents, and hostility or indifference to God and the church among those on the outside commonly follow arrested growth. Effective witness requires communicating the faith to the children of members so that they learn to love Jesus Christ in their early childhood and accept His teachings without going

27

astray. It requires also dealing in brotherly love with those on the outside, commending the Savior to them, and trying by all means to bring them to Christian faith, experience, and purpose. To fail with either the children in Christian homes or with adults and children on the outside is to retard the work of God and is, therefore, tragic in the extreme.

Focusing attention first on children of members, we see that many never become convinced that the church is of God or that Jesus is the Savior of the world. They do not acquire in childhood a consciousness of God. They often enter adult life and assume responsibilities of citizenship and parenthood without ever giving serious consideration to the meaning, obligations, and privileges of discipleship. The blessings that have come to them through Christ Jesus are not appreciated. They may even be admitted to church membership (this often happens in a shockingly casual way) without experiencing more than an inoculation with a mild type of Christian thought that actually prevents dedication.

Contributing to the tragedy of retarded church growth through neglect of the children is a confused antisocial dogma of extreme individualism which makes parents reluctant to teach their children the Christian faith. "My children must make their own decisions about Christ and the church," say parents. "I will not force my beliefs on them." In refraining from teaching Christianity to their children they in fact, though unintentionally, teach irreligion.

Another contribution to the tragedy of retardation is made by parents who ignore religion in the home but, from a sense of guilt or for some other reason, send their children to Sunday school, while themselves not attending. When to this failure they add neglect of worship in church services, they say with actions that speak louder than words that the Christian religion may be real but certainly is unimportant.

The criminal delinquency of many children reflects their association with churches that are not growing because they have ceased to practice and prove the gospel. The children regard the teaching of the church as untrue because they have not seen it confirmed in their homes or communities. They take little interest in the church when it takes little interest in them and meets for them no felt need. Delinquent nongrowing churches and delinquent parents naturally produce delinquent children. Churches that give the children in their midst the loving attention that Jesus gave to children do not produce delinquents or allow many to be produced within the circle of their influence. The growth of the church is helped by the accession of children to membership, and delinquent adults and adolescents are often brought to penitence and pardon by the influence of the life and witness of those children. A successful pastor said: "We have won many parents through their children." Isaiah's prophecy that "a little child shall lead them" has been fulfilled many times.

Tragic retardation of church growth has also been caused by communicating the faith only to those who are connected in some way with the church. Many congregations have developed admirable official programs for their own children and young people but have done little to reach out into the surrounding area to win others. History provides numerous examples of the tragic effects that follow naturally when church growth is retarded. One of these comes from Arabia, where the church through several centuries failed to grow with reasonable rapidity.

Congregational worship services never became popular in the Arabian church. Little groups of professing Christians lived in the midst of pagan tribes, but no effective ministry of the Word and the Sacraments was established. The Scriptures, studied reverently elsewhere, were never much known in Arabia. The instruction Jesus gave: Teach "them to observe all that I have commanded you," was generally ignored. Basic truth was forgotten and superstition flourished. The church grew only in weakness and age as year after year went by. Then Islam was born out of the unmet longings of pagan peoples for vital religion. A neglected and neglectful church became emaciated and anemic and at length died not so much a victim of Islamic aggression as of its own failure to disciple the tribes of its land.

Nearby North Africa about A.D. 500 provides a second example. There a once-flourishing church failed to maintain an effective program of evangelism and religious education. It neglected entirely the Berber villages and failed to communicate Christian faith, concern, and purpose to the children within the homes of professed believers. Godliness declined and evil flourished. Bishops fought one another for top places in the church. Instead of healing the sick and meeting all sorts of human need, as Jesus had taught his disciples to do, these ambitious church leaders vied with one another in mortifying the flesh, practicing austerities, lauding physical weakness as an aid to holiness, and even renouncing human society, all acts repugnant to the spirit of Jesus and to the apostolic church. These acts undoubtedly reflect the influence of Hindu-Buddhist thought which was in those centuries much stronger in the Middle East and North Africa than Western scholarship has yet recognized. The evils against which Jesus preached and worked were actually promoted in his name and the good he did was, by implication, accounted evil. A warning against normal living and a call for asceticism were substituted for the gospel of God's love for man, even sinful man, and for the abundant life which Jesus had promised. So when Islam arrived in North Africa it was welcomed by throngs of Berber idolaters whose needs the church had ignored. And hereditary Christians, divided and weakened by strife, uninstructed or wrongly taught, lacked the strength to resist the fervent effort of the Arabian iconoclasts and the grace and wisdom to defend the gospel.

Many centuries ago the church that traces its origin to the labors of the apostle Thomas in South India grew rapidly in numerical strength and in spiritual power. While its Christian attainment is not easily measured, especially after the passing of nearly sixty generations, tradition represents that church in South India as being an example of holy living, devotion, and missionary zeal. It underwent persistent persecution and produced a long line of trusted and beloved priests, bishops, and martyrs. Such scriptures as were available were reverently studied and expounded. Orderly and righteous church government, regular congregational worship, and high standards of moral conduct were established. Every vestige of idolatry was eliminated, despite the fact that idolatry was highly prevalent among neighbors of the Christians, and had been the common practice of Christians themselves before their conversion. During this period conversions continued despite severe and unrelenting persecution. The blood of the martyrs, there as in Asia Minor and in Europe, proved to be the seed of the church.

But in time members of the church longed for freedom from persecution. On condition that they be allowed to bring up their

31

children in the Christian faith, they made an agreement with the Hindu king to refrain from calling for or accepting converts from the Hindus. The agreement brought an immediate end to persecution and in time Christians achieved a very privileged position socially and economically, but it came perilously near to destroying the church. Hinduism has an unrivaled absorptive power. Repeatedly in its history it has absorbed other groups with which it has maintained contact for a long time. It very nearly absorbed that nonevangelizing church. Competent students have suggested that only the arrival of missionaries from outside India saved this ancient church of South India from a like fate. Be that as it may, this church has now reclaimed its former strength and is today a powerful force for evangelism in democratic India where religious liberty is enjoyed as a right, guaranteed by the constitution of the republic. Missionaries of rare devotion and skill from that revitalized church proclaim Christ in other parts of India and in the adjoining kingdom of Nepal, only recently opened to the work of the church.

Contemporary examples of retarded church growth are found in many widely scattered areas where major population shifts have occurred. They have taken members and familiar people away and have brought into the neighborhood of the church new and strange folk. Wherever that has happened a difficult adjustment has been needed, and too frequently it has not been made. The church has often concentrated upon existing members and people like them and made little effort to reach new residents of another language, race, or religion.

Differences of language, race, color, custom, occupation, and even social and economic status have been accepted as barriers to friendship and to the brotherly love that gives power and effectiveness to evangelism and cohesion to church fellowship. Every one of these differences can be, and often has been, overcome in the service of God. Overcoming them indeed makes the church stronger in every way. When any of these differences is allowed to bar the way to helpfulness, tragedy results. It begins in the hearts of those who are neglected and reaches into every aspect of community life.

Some churches that have moved from inner-city locations to suburbs seem to have given little thought to the effect of their removal upon those whom they have left behind. Social workers often encounter intense resentment and strong-grievance reactions. "They give money to foreign heathens but for us they don't give a thought," said a Negro in Boston. He came from a Southern Protestant background but complained about Protestant abandonment of Negro-infiltrated areas in Boston and praised the work of a Catholic congregation that stayed and increased its staff in order to help the newcomers.

In many American cities wide areas exist where once there were many strong, flourishing Protestant churches but now are only a few struggling congregations. Yet in the neighborhood of these surviving churches are large groups of unchurched people living in almost pagan darkness. It should not be necessary to argue the case of the tragedy of the defeated church among neglected people. People are essentially the same everywhere, regardless of race, language, color, or any of the many barriers that have been allowed to restrict fellowship and thus to interfere with church growth. Every man's deepest and most urgent needs are those which he shares with the whole race of man, not those that concern him as a white man or a Negro, a poor man or a rich man, an illiterate or a doctor of philosophy, an American or a Mexican. If the church has meaning only for Americans or only for privileged English-speaking people, it is not necessary to anyone's welfare now or in the world to come. But since the message Christ Jesus gave to his church is of infinite importance to every individual whatever his color, condition, or creed, it is necessary to all men everywhere.

The church has no authority to revise the mandate to preach, teach, and propagate the gospel, to change its message about God and man, or to limit the company of those to whom it is presented. No nation can opt out of the family of God and the church cannot rightly exclude any nation, race, tribe, or people from its field of service. To deny the need of any people for the gospel is to deny Christ and to deny Christ is to compound tragedy.

A Sikh resident in California since boyhood, a Hindu merchant who has run a store in Panama for twenty years, a Chinese shoemaker in a city in India, and an African medical student in London are among the many who in one recent six-month period complained to this writer that they have been in contact with Christian people for years but have never been invited to join a church or been made to feel certain that they would be welcome at its services.

Mahatma Gandhi talked frequently and freely about having been very near a public confession of Christian faith and a request for baptism and church membership when practicing law in South Africa. He went to a church where a renowned minister was to preach. Arriving late, after the ushers had left the doors, he quietly entered and sat down. Soon an usher came and said quite politely: "I beg your pardon but colored people are not invited to worship here." As Mr. Gandhi reported the incident, the ensuing conversation went like this: Mr. Gandhi: "Well, that doesn't matter. I've come without an invitation. Let's not interrupt the worship."

The usher: "But you don't understand; I have to ask you to leave."

Mr. Gandhi: "That wouldn't be reverent. I can't leave while the service is in progress."

The usher withdrew but returned with the head usher who then spoke: "You don't understand. Colored people are not invited to these services."

Mr. Gandhi: "I understand perfectly." 1226925

Head usher: "But you are not leaving!"

Mr. Gandhi: "No, I can't do that now. But when the service is over, I'll leave and I promise that I'll never come back."

I had the privilege of knowing Mr. Gandhi for over twenty-five years and of meeting him frequently. He mentioned this incident to me several times and admitted that it strongly affected his thinking about the church. No one can appraise with certain knowledge the tragic influences of those ushers' words or of the more basic sin of that congregation's racial policy. But it is essentially the policy of hundreds of segregated congregations in the world of today, and their current actions may produce even more extensive tragedy than the loss to the church of the growth which the conversion of the great Mahatma might have brought about.

It is characteristic of retarded people that they have difficulty in diagnosing their condition or prescribing suitably or accepting the prescriptions of others for it. That is as true of spiritual as of mental or physical retardations. The man whom others know as proud may regard himself as notably humble. A woman regarded by her neighbors as rude, inconsiderate, and negligent may esteem herself as an example of decorous behavior. No task any of us sets himself is easier than self-deception, and because it is so easy it is a popular pastime. Authorities tell us that often the critic is most severe in his judgment of others when he attributes to them faults that he knows are peculiarly his own.

Use of this projection pattern is not confined to individuals but is often adopted by whole groups. Communists attack the Western Powers for the very reasons for which the Western Powers attack Communists. White councils accuse Negroes of doing exactly what, in their own behavior, gives most offense to Negroes. In the post-partition disturbances in India and Pakistan, during which more people were killed than in most declared wars, the Hindus and Sikhs on the one side and the Moslems on the other justified their crimes as "retaliation" and necessary to restrain the other side from further excesses. Attacks upon colonialism have often proved preludes to attempts to set up local regimes of tyranny.

Retarded individuals and groups need to repent rather than to justify themselves. Jesus called insistently for people to repent. He promised forgiveness and a new birth to the penitent. The new life in Christ Jesus is begun with confession, repentance, and conversion. It is injured and severely jeopardized by unconfessed wrongdoing, by rationalized excuses, by tolerated faults in one's self that are denounced in others, by unabashed insensitiveness to the needs and interests of others, and by exaggerated concern for one's own selfish advantages. Emphasis on repentance and conversion benefits men and promotes church growth.

Modern psychology has rediscovered the therapeutic value of

36

confession but some of its humanistic practitioners have become entangled in self-made webs of speculation about how to remove the sense of guilt without seeking God's help. There is no substitute for the conversion experience that is at the center of the gospel that Jesus proclaimed and charged his disciples to communicate to all nations. Too many people today are trying to get rid of their sense of guilt by talking to psychiatrists at so much per hour, instead of talking to God at the cost or repentance and confession. Pure psychology is an asset of the Kingdom, as is all truth, and those practitioners who in its name try to eliminate God from the human scene should restudy the issue with which they deal. Suave speech may make an easy conquest of disturbed minds but it cannot take the place of the grace of God in lifting the burden of sin and transforming character. Let those psychiatrists who have been setting themselves against God and his church recognize and confess the error of their ways and begin to use their talents and skills, as wiser members of the profession are already doing, to express the love of God in healing the sick! To deprive their patients of the help of religious faith is very unfair to them. A high proportion of those whom Jesus healed in Galilee and Judea were mentally disturbed people. Such people were said then, in Palestine, to have evil spirits. That is the explanation given by many people in much of the world today for the complaints for which the more enlightened consult the psychiatrists.

The unmet spiritual needs of church members impede the growth of the church, in much the same way that the obviously unmet health needs of his patients limit the growth of a physician's practice. But it does not follow that only perfect Christians can promote the growth of the church. A patient who bears witness to the understanding, kindness, and skill of his doctor, who is apparently improving in health, or who seems to have been cured of an illness may influence others to come to his physician. Likewise the church member who believes fervently in Jesus Christ, speaks of him in loving words and deeds, and gives evidence of an improved life as a result of becoming his disciple may draw others to him.

Communicating the good news about Christ to others, being an obligation of discipleship, is necessary to the spiritual well-being of the church member. If only saints could make the church grow, the church would come to a sad end in a few decades. By which time the saints would all be dead! But by helping others to come to Christ sinners move toward sainthood. Andrew knew only a little about Jesus when he brought his brother Simon to him. Papa Gonjolo of the Congo, telling the story of his life, said: "I was only about 10 per cent converted when I began working for the conversion of others. Had I never brought others to Christ, I would never have been more than a 10 per cent Christian." In bringing others to Christ this first-generation Congolese Christian has become a near saint, immensely respected and loved by thousands in the Congo and other countries in and out of Africa.

Angrahit, a convert to Christ from among the lowly Dhusiya Chamars in India said: "When I confessed faith in Christ as my Savior I thought mostly of salvation from poverty and oppression. And that salvation I have obtained by his grace. I used to be hungry most of the time, and so were my wife and children. God saved me from drinking and gambling, and then I was able to get enough food for all the family. But salvation means ten times more now. God has forgiven my sins, taken away my fear, removed my superstition, and given me faith and hope and purpose. If I could not have known Jesus before I understood his salvation I could never have known him, for it was by knowing him that understanding came." Not only was Angrahit's life given new meaning and a quality of glory previously unknown, but his wife shared the new meaning and the glory. Together they brought many others to Christ and helped to establish the church in a wide area around their home. Their children and grandchildren are now educated, patriotic citizens of the new India, bringing many to Christian faith, and honored by all who know them. But until Angrahit's conversion no one in that family line for a thousand years had been able to read and none had been concerned for the salvation of his fellowmen, for they were despised outcastes.

One can only understand the tragedy of the retarded church by studying it against the background of a well-developed church. Seeing what God has done through a Papa Gonjolo or an Angrahit, one thinks of what might have been in thousands of places to the incalcuable good of millions of needy people had the church won others who were just as accessible, and might have been just as responsive, had they learned of the Savior.

One chief reason for retarded growth is sheer complacency. People take too much satisfaction in having realized a minor good and do not even try to achieve the major good to which God is calling them. A pastor and his lay colleagues in the officiary of a church, satisfied with the moderate giving to missions of previous years, make a perfunctory call for a missionary offering and the uninstructed, uninspired, unchallenged congregation make a grumbling response that equals or perhaps slightly raises the level of previous giving. The pastor and the church

39

officials congratulate themselves and the congregation when the offering could and should have been several times as much as it was. And because so much less than their best has been done for the Kingdom, the church loses much of the blessing it needs for its own life and fails to accomplish the larger part of the good it should do for others.

There are across the earth, without question, many who would have been zealous Christians had they been reached by missions. Instead they are getting along badly without Christ. For them life could have been rich, exciting, and wonderful but is instead poor, drab, and frustrating. And knowing only the kind of religion their fathers knew before them, exploited by priests and tyrants, hungry and friendless, with no idea of the difference Christ could make in their lives, they are wide open to Communist deception and conquest.

Another major reason for retarded growth is divisiveness within the church. Division is bad but divisiveness is worse. When people learn of Christ and begin to consider whether they should turn to him, they naturally look at the church and are often deterred by what they see. "I decided to become a Christian but was warned by all my friends not to become a Catholic and by some of them not to join any of the three churches I most liked. So for fear that I might join the wrong church, I remained a Hindu." Thus spoke an eminent Indian national leader. Another even more influential leader of India said: "When the Churches solve their own problems of division, I'll believe they can help us solve our urgent national problems."

The ill effects of the divisions among Christians are by no means limited to their impact upon the minds of non-Christians. They include wastefulness, isolation, and misdirection of effort

40

because valuable lessons of experience have not been shared. The duplication of effort growing out of ecclesiastical separation causes considerable waste. In one area in India three hospitals have been run by three different missionary societies within eleven miles of one another. Each has been understaffed and poorly equipped. This does not make sense but wastes dollars and reduces the effectiveness of the service that might have been rendered in a united hospital.

Yet good stewardship calls for more than a union of service efforts; it requires a sharing of understanding, a fellowship of prayer and praise, a community of purpose and plan, a oneness in love and loyalty. Surely all of these are comprehended in the prayer of our Lord when approaching Calvary, as reported by John: "I do not pray for these only, but also for those who are to believe in me through their word, that they may all be one; even as thou, Father, art in me and I in thee, that they also may be in us, so that the world may believe that thou hast sent me."

The tragedies of isolation and misdirection are not always averted by union, but their frequency and severity are reduced. Within an isolated church or mission, programs are often founded on assumptions that have been completely disproved within the experience of other churches and missions working in comparable conditions. Because there is little or no communication between church leaders, one knows little or nothing about the experiences of the others, or what is worse, knows only what is not true—the deposited debris of rumor and conjecture. Full exchange of understandings would make possible immense reinforcement of church growth.

As an example, a certain church had been at work in a wide area in India for seventy-five years, yet the resultant Christian

41

community had fewer than one hundred members. Its program was based on certain assumptions mistakenly called principles, which were proved wrong by the experience of other churches working in comparable conditions in adjoining areas. One of those assumptions was that the motives of educated, "respectable" people who desired to become Christians would likely be good, but the motives of the uneducated lower classes would have to be purified during a long period of testing. Acting on that assumption this particular church let a few questionable, upper-caste people come in and take it over. But they kept many earnest, low-caste seekers after God out of the fellowship until one by one, in discouragement, they gave up the quest. Disappointment with the upper-caste people whom they had received was—by a strange perversity from which good people are not always "saved"—used to bolster belief in the wisdom of holding off the lower classes.

Eventually, however, the facts about the experience of other churches became known through personal contact and definite inquiry, and the old assumptions had to be abandoned. A new attitude toward the more responsive lower classes produced in a half-dozen years more converts and apparently better Christians than had resulted from seventy-five years of faithfully following the old mistaken assumption. A veteran churchman who had spent three decades working eagerly with the upper classes and avoiding the lower classes was so changed by two years under the new policy that he talked sadly of the "wasted years before my colleagues and I began to question our own superior goodness and wisdom, and discovered that there were good and wise missionaries and national Christians, from whom we could learn much, in other churches."

42

Instances of retarded growth in church membership and spiritual development are by no means limited to primitive cultures or poor people. They are possibly even more numerous in areas of plenty and among the highly privileged. People who have within their reach every cultural opportunity and are members of a church but who are without a continuing Christian purpose are spiritually retarded people. What they are is terribly different from what they might be, by God's grace. They inflict upon themselves the destructive boredom of devotion to the trivial when they might have known the enduring joy of working together with God for his eternal kingdom. Long-retarded nominal Christians may become, by God's grace, dedicated disciples, working with God to establish his kingdom within their own hearts, homes, and neighborhoods, and throughout the world.

While rejoicing that the tragedy of retarded growth in the individual and in the corporate life of the church can be overcome, we dare not lay aside the responsibility to do all within our power as individuals and as members of local congregations and groups of Christians to stimulate growth everywhere. One of the most distinctive marks of Christian discipleship is the readiness to accept personal and group responsibilities. If all who love Jesus Christ and believe in him will begin to do the utmost God puts within their power to do, the church will grow in spiritual and numerical strength to the immense benefit of all mankind.

III

Assembled Lessons from Many Lands

At least four early disciples of Jesus decided to assemble records of what he said and did. To those records a grateful church has given the name "The Gospels." The sermons of those disciples are forgotten but their reports on Jesus are read every day on every continent and on many islands. They provide most of our materials for studying the life and teachings of the Master and for enriching our spiritual life.

Luke wrote a second report dealing chiefly with the rapid growth of the church in Jerusalem after the ascension of Jesus when multitudes declared their faith and were added to the fellowship of believers; with the labors of Peter; and with the story of Saul, his persecution of the church, his conversion and transformation into Paul, and his planting of many churches in Asia Minor and Greece.

One might pen an eloquent lament, in prose or poetry, that comparable records of the growth of the church in every land and age are not available now. How much it would have meant if other men, with faith and love and the insights they give, had written like accounts of the labors of the other apostles, of the developing life and expansion of the church, and of the multiplication of disciples which they under God brought about! How valuable it might be, for example, if we knew what lessons Thomas learned in India; if it was indeed he, as so many there believe, who first preached the gospel in that great subcontinent below the Himalayas!

Why did not disciples of succeeding generations record with the same meticulous care as Matthew, Mark, Luke, and John what they knew about the growth of the church? How much it might help the young missionary or the prospective missionary in training if he could study records of church expansion in every generation as luminous and as credible as the book of Acts! And what it might mean in the crises of our times if there were available to the whole church all the lessons that God has taught to groups of disciples here and there in every age! Many valuable lessons learned at great cost have undoubtedly been forgotten and lost beyond the hope of recovery, but others are locked up in denominational or geographical compartments. A great opportunity awaits the effort of serious students to assemble these lessons and make them generally available to the expanding world church.

A far from exhaustive study of records and situations in churches and missions in India convinced me years ago that grave mistakes have been made in determining and maintaining policies. and procedures without studying the records of earlier efforts. Many assumptions on which pioneer missionaries worked proved to be tragically wrong and were revised. Nevertheless new missions—often of the younger churches—and even new missionaries within the same mission have often acted on those erroneous assumptions until they have been disproved afresh within their own experience.

Our Lord challenged many assumptions on which the religious professionals of Israel were acting in his day. And he declared the love of God with the mind to be a part of the first and greatest commandment. His disciples are under obligation to show themselves approved unto God. Their field of study in regard to the establishment of churches cannot rightly be restricted to the Scriptures or so defined as to leave out the areas of experience.

John R. Mott, undoubtedly the greatest of modern missionary statesmen, said to a young missionary, "Challenge the assumptions on which you are asked to work. If a careful study convinces you that they are correct, follow them faithfully. If, however, you are then convinced that they are wrong, try either to revise or abandon them. Do not repeat proven errors!"

One assumption which early missionaries in India made, and to which succeeding generations clung tenaciously, was that the new convert should be separated from his former associates and made to live in the company of Christians while being indoctrinated and freed from erroneous old beliefs and harmful habits. It was a disastrous mistake. It separated the new believers from friends and loved ones and made them socially, and to some extent spiritually, dependent upon people of another race and culture. It caused many converts to experience social dislocation and made their relatives and neighbors resentful and hostile.

It is sometimes claimed that the separation of the convert from his relatives was not due to the initiative of the missionary but to the unwillingness of high-caste Hindus and Moslems to allow the convert to remain at home. Non-Christians, however, say that hostility to conversion grew out of resentment over the withdrawal of converts from their families. Which came first, the withdrawal of the convert at the missionary's initiative or the expulsion of the convert by his family, is debatable. In any case it is clear that missionaries generally welcomed the break and only isolated efforts were made by converts and a few dissenting missionaries to assert the new believer's right to remain in his home and there bear witness to Christ.

In contrast to that assumption of value in separation and the practice built upon it, Jesus said: "The kingdom of God . . . is like leaven which a woman took and hid in three measures of meal, till it was all leavened." In harmony with his Lord's teaching Paul stayed with those whom he led to Christ and helped them present the gospel to their neighbors and kinfolk. But the isolation of the convert on the mission compound removed the leaven from society and hurt the convert, his family, his neighbors, and the church.

This lesson, perhaps most clearly taught in India, has value for missionaries in every part of today's world. Observation in other countries of Asia, Africa, Latin America, and the islands of the Pacific has shown the author that this mistake has been repeated very widely, and is even now being made by earnest people who have failed to learn from experience of others.

A second lesson, which this writer learned in India and has found confirmed in observations in many countries, is that the foreign missionary, by virtue of being foreign, experiences many handicaps in presenting the gospel. Some of these handicaps can easily and without awareness be communicated to those with whom he becomes associated in faith and service. When the church seems to be foreign and strange, few people in any land or culture can be entirely free from prejudice against it and its message. Seeming foreignness among one's own countrymen may be especially offensive. Theodore Roosevelt before

World War I thundered against "hyphenated Americans," and ardent patriots in many lands have passionately denounced those of their countrymen who in becoming Christians have seemed to become foreigners and to lose their sense of nationality and community.

In these conditions wisdom demands that the missionary, if he is to be effective in persuading men to become disciples of Christ, be more than normally self-effacing and given to the practice of preferring others to himself and his kind for office and honor in the church. This the missionary finds difficult. Because he has convictions and holds to them strongly, he is likely to consider that his leadership is necessary to the well-being of the church. Clearly—and this lesson has been convincingly taught in many countries—the foreign missionary must either become integrated in the citizenry of the country in which he serves or help to produce and train citizens to take over his duties with all possible speed. It will help the missionary who labors outside of his homeland and his supporters to understand this issue: if they will ask themselves how well they think the church in their own homelands would prosper if its leadership were, to any considerable extent, foreign or if positions of major importance were reserved for foreigners.

However dedicated a missionary may be, and however pure his motives, he may without intent or awareness teach and spread much that is not a part of the gospel of Christ, or even be compatible with it. Enemies have denounced missions as agents of imperialism. Some have withheld support because they have regarded missions as organized interference with religion and culture in other lands. These are inept criticisms, but a wise missionary will recognize that in many aspects of his personality he is a product of his time and culture. He may be justly proud of some features of the life and record of his country and thoroughly ashamed of other features. But he must remember that he is not a missionary for his country. His task is to make disciples of Jesus, not to remake those to whom he ministers into the likeness of his countrymen. Most missionaries are extraordinarily patriotic and their experience abroad may enhance their appreciation of their homeland. But they should never identify the kingdom of God with the military, political, or other interests of their own country. To do so is to place obstacles on the road by which they hope to lead others to God.

Channels of communication opened for preaching or otherwise presenting the gospel serve inevitably to spread other influences as well. Study is needed of what may be described either as parasitic or stowaway forces that make use of Christian missions and thus slow down the liberating program of the church. The missionary has often opened the whole realm of reading and writing to a previously illiterate people, or he has been the first to use printing in a national or regional language. But once the people have learned to read and are hungry for printed materials, then evil-minded politicians exploiting hatred and prejudice or even vicious purveyors of pornography and ruthless Communist preachers of atheism may outbid the disciples of Jesus for the attention of the new readers. Even now while Christian agencies in several areas are pleading in vain for resources to implement literature programs prepared to meet felt needs, the Communists and the producers of obscene writings and pictures are rushing to poison heart and mind with hate and filth. Adequate support of a well-conceived and -directed Chris-

49

tian literature program would do much to insure rapid growth of the church in many lands. Positive Christian teaching and creative writing on any phase of social welfare provide effective defenses against Communism. What is essential for the entire church in a wide area is often left undone because the resources available are assigned instead to purposes that serve only local or denominational interests.

The accusation is made that such noncommendable Western social customs as extravagance, accentuation of sex in dress, use of alcoholic liquors in social functions, runaway marriages, easy divorces, and contempt for tradition are spread by increased contact between Western and Eastern nations. And as Christian missions are responsible for much intercultural contact and the interpenetration of cultures they are held partly responsible for the global growth of these evil customs. Few people would accuse missionaries of purposely and directly aiding in the spreading of unhelpful customs. In fact they are often criticized by less strict Christian moralists for uncompromising opposition to some or all of these behavior patterns. Yet the man or woman who responds most cordially to the missionary, for that very reason, may be most strongly influenced by the missionary's countryman who also comes as a Christian, but who may be only a nominal Christian or even an unwholesome character. From such a one the convert may acquire a new social pattern that includes one, some, or all of those objectionable social customs.

These considerations inspire appeals to two categories of Christian believers; those who are citizens of non-Christian lands, and those who go to such lands either to work or as tourists. The recognition of the difficulties that beset professional missionaries working in lands of which they are not citizens imposes upon both categories acceptance of major responsibilities for the growth of the church.

Only harm results if evangelistic effort is not made at all or is reduced in amount or quality because the missionary is handicapped in doing it. It is far better for the church to grow under missionary initiative and leadership than for it to decline or to remain stationary. But better by far is the maximum growth which can be achieved through a full partnership of local Christians and missionary representatives of the wider church. National Christians in many situations need to face the fact that a tragic retardation of church growth began in their neighborhood years ago and persists still. A radical change can be brought about if local Christians and available associates use all their resources in preaching and proving the gospel.

The responsibility of Christians temporarily resident among non-Christians calls for emphatic statement; many instances are known of people being converted through the witness of Christians with whom they have come into contact outside the church and its institutions. A Sikh civilian prisoner of war in a Japanese camp in Malaya came to Christian faith and confession through association with other prisoners. He saw a vast difference in his fellow prisoners, and careful study convinced him that Christians who really believed in Christ had something he and all men needed. In an out-of-the-way village in South India a group of aboriginal tribespeople are devout Christians because a convert whose people turned against him came among them and made himself useful in many ways. They fed him and helped him construct a small hut. He read the Bible to them, prayed with them, and did whatever he could to help them. Before they met an ordained minister and could be baptized they were fervent in faith and regular in worship.

Many Christians temporarily resident in predominantly non-Christian communities have united with local congregations in maintaining churches or establishing new ones and in the support of schools, hospitals, and other service programs. An increasing number of lay Christians try to be in fact nonprofessional missionaries. These men and women may be doing more and better than they know or suspect. They may soon be recognized as pioneers of a new and very effective order of missionaries.

A fact discovered in every study of church growth in Asia, Africa, South America, and the island world is that religious faith spreads from person to person and group to group. This fact provided the title for Donald McGavran's invaluable book, *The Bridges of God*, and is the basic reason for the development of group and people movements to Christian discipleship, even where missionaries have been afraid of group action in religion. This calls for a new study of the methods of Jesus and of his mandate to his disciples.

When Christ chose his first disciples and began training them for responsibilities in his church he chose a group of men, not just twelve individuals. All of them were Jews and at least ten, and possibly eleven, were Galilean Jews. This was in a multi-racial, multicreedal society. And he trained them as a group. During this training he confined them to work with their own people. They were expressly forbidden to go to others. And during most of their training they were in the general area of their homes, among relatives and neighbors. The disciple who was less completely one of their group than any other was Judas, who betrayed the Master.

When the training of these disciples was complete, Jesus entrusted his church entirely to them. Called to meet him on a mountaintop in Galilee these eleven made the long and difficult trip there. When they beheld him they fell at his feet in joyful adoration. Yet some doubted even then, says Matthew. Jesus did not upbraid them for their pre-crucifixion desertion or post-resurrection doubt but he made of the occasion a commissioning service. He charged them as a group to go to groups with the gospel. "Make disciples of nations," Matthew reports him as saying, not: "Make a few disciples in every nation," as some seem to think that he meant to say, or at least should have said.

Normal people need one another's help in religion as in other aspects of life. All of us require social support to live the good life. The idea that the vital obligations of religion can be met only by individuals in private is more compatible with Hinduism and Buddhism than with Christianity, which is social in its essence. Congregational worship is at the center of Christian living. An individual cannot be in right relations with God and in wrong relations with people. Jesus taught us to associate even our prayers for forgiveness with our practice of forgiveness. "He who does not love his brother whom he has seen, cannot love God whom he has not seen." The current strong objection to the social gospel among some fervent Christians, in so far as it is valid, is based upon the failure of some who emphasize service in Christ's name to relate that service, as Jesus did, to the call for penitence, the invitation to believe, and the promise of pardon. Jesus never neglected spiritual needs while healing the sick. And while saying, "Seek ye first the kingdom of God, and His righteousness" (K.J.V.), he never put off physical needs until spiritual needs had been met. "He makes his sun rise on the evil and on the good, and sends rain on the just and on the unjust."

Doing good to needy people is an obligation for Christians but it is certainly not the only obligation. No amount of social work takes the place of proclaiming Christ as Lord and Savior and persuading men to become his disciples. One of the most urgent duties now is to effectively relate the numerous service agencies of the church to evangelism and church growth. Service agencies that are concerned only with meeting felt physical needs, and refrain deliberately—for any reason—from teaching religion as Christ taught it, and from calling for allegiance to Christ, have no valid claim to the Christian name.

In international thinking about missions two widely held theories seem to be based upon assumptions that have been disproved. One of these may be called the geographical occupation theory. It is built on the assumption that the location of a number of mission stations in strategic places is the best way to produce a church. But experience proves that mission stations do not always produce churches. On the contrary the building of a mission station may actually retard the development of the church. One reason for this is that it locates available resources before discovering where the best opportunity for fruitful service exists. In Asia, Africa, and Latin America the records show repeatedly that openings of very great promise have been neglected because the missionary staff was committed and engaged elsewhere. Often a school is opened in the hope that it will be a direct evangelizing agency. But it makes such demands on the time of the missionary that when a group of people ten, twenty, or thirty miles away becomes interested in the gospel and invites the missionary to come and live among them, teaching them from day to day the way Paul did in founding churches in Asia Minor and in Greece, he is unable to respond.

Sometimes a missionary who has resolved to devote himself entirely to direct evangelism is invited to help an isolated group of people who desire to become Christians. But he does not respond because he has purchased a house some distance away and feels that he must continue to occupy it to protect it against thieves. He tries in vain to start a church near where he lives by occasional visits to people nearer his home than are those who are asking for his help.

The preservation of mobility for the missionary and the resources at his command is far more important than the residential occupation of strategic centers. The great missionary opportunities come when one person or a group accepts Christ and yet remains in normal, friendly relations with relatives and neighbors, inviting or welcoming the help of the missionary in Christian discipleship. Then the missionary teaches and preaches the gospel, and helps the new local believer or believers to apply the teachings of Christ to their own lives, and to interpret them to their neighbors. The new convert, when he responds heartily to the claims of Christ, excites the interest of his relatives and friends in Christ. The missionary could not possibly, unaided, influence the community so much, but he can, through the new convert, exercise a potent influence for evangelism. That is the great opportunity—to reinforce the influence of the local believer. In no country have I been able to find a vigorous, well-established church, exercising a strong influence on the nation, except where local converts have become so vibrantly and radiantly Christian that they have commended the gospel to others. The missionary task is to win converts and help them to realize and meet their responsibilities to evangelize their countrymen. When missions lose sight of that fact and give priority to mission stations and mission residences in strategic centers, the effect is a tragic retardation of church growth.

The other theory is that years of seed-sowing are normal and even necessary and should not occasion distress. What seeming support for this assumption has been found in either Scripture or agriculture is not clear. The theory is certainly erroneous and has retarded the growth of the church. It operates to prevent immediate maximum effort. When a missionary's faith is set for delayed action it is almost inevitable that the people to whom he presents the gospel will sense that he does not expect them to respond at once. It is as though he were saying: "Repent and believe, but not now; I'm only sowing the seed. We'll expect to harvest the crop some years hence."

It is easier to bring people from the background of another religion to Christian discipleship when the gospel is presented to them in expectation of an immediate or very early acceptance. Talk about being converted at some future date may not be entirely ineffective but it certainly does discourage early decision. In India non-Christians in opposing the church have made effective use of the fact that large numbers of people are rarely converted where they have known Christianity a long time. More often it is where the church and missions are new and help people to a quick decision that the most converts are made. In two countries of Africa somewhat similar arguments were put to the writer by unconverted pagans. One of them said: "There is no likelihood of conversions in that region. The people there have become accustomed to Christians whom they do not like, and who apparently do not like them." Another declared: "Christianity is an old story here. We have heard it preached all our lives and it doesn't interest us. Only those like it to whom it is news."

For the great advances in church growth so urgently needed today all over the world, increased mobility and a livelier expectation of immediate results are required. Freedom from the aforementioned assumptions will certainly help. This phraseology is just another way of pleading for wise stewardship and active faith.

When Jesus talked to the Samaritan woman of ill repute at Jacob's well, he saw an opportunity to bring her to God and used it to produce immediate results of large dimensions. Seeing that his disciples, on their return with food from the village, had no idea of what he had accomplished in talking with this woman and had no expectations of early results for the Kingdom from their ministry or his, he said to them, "Do you not say, 'There are yet four months, then comes the harvest'? I tell you, lift up your eyes, and see how the fields are already white for harvest."

That immoral woman, who had come to the well in the middle of the day to escape the taunts of other women, made a quick response to Jesus and a remarkable change took place in her immediately. She came, eager to escape observation. After talking with Jesus she went back to the village calling for attention, eager to tell about Jesus. Her conversion was not complete, for as eager as she was to talk about this wonderful Man, she did not restrict herself to the truth. She said that Jesus had told her everything she had ever done. That certainly was not true. She was, from the human point of view, an unlikely prospect for conversion. But she not only underwent an immediate, radical change but became an agent of God for effecting a wonderful change for good in the life of her village. Hearing her, many went to the well to hear him and on their invitation he and the twelve stayed in the village for two days. Some believed in him because of what she had told them. Others believed when they themselves heard him and said: "We know that this is indeed the Savior of the world."

These lessons from the ministry of Jesus are repeated in the experience of the church time and time again. Yet many good people, eager to serve God, continue to labor without the expectation of early results. In India the writer was often told by ministers that they were working in a very difficult condition, among hardhearted, unresponsive people, where as many conversions could not be expected as in other areas. Yet it was often clear that the chief obstacle to success in obtaining conversions and church growth in their locality was their own lack of faith. So long as they did not believe that people around them could be converted, God himself could not effect conversions through their efforts.

John R. Mott once remarked that he knew a number of people who were always filled with enthusiasm about their work and obtained excellent results; but others who were never happy in their assignments, were always sure that very little could be accomplished therein, made little effort, and never got good results. Dr. Mott had a technique for getting information that would help him appraise an applicant for an important post.

58

He began by asking the man to tell him the five most serious difficulties he had encountered in his work, and then to report the five greatest encouragements he had experienced. If the encouragements were emphasized he was at once favorable toward that man. If one is accustomed to focus his attention on difficulties and evils with which he has to contend rather than on God and his work he will likely achieve little. But if he sees God at work and is enthusiastic about working with him, he will accomplish much. Only if one lifts up his eyes and sees the fields white unto the harvest is he likely to go forth prepared to reap and bring in the sheaves. All across the world today where people are free in the broadest sense they can be won to Christ by men and women who combine faith with understanding and love.

Another lesson, learned independently in many countries, deserves the attention of all who love the Lord Jesus and share his love for the nations. This is the terrible prevalence of fear outside the Christian fellowship and its disappearance inside. Many tribal groups live under the tyranny of fear all their lives. A former village woman in Pakistan, now working as an evangelist, said: "If you were born in a mature, instructed Christian home you cannot imagine the terror in which I lived as a girl. I was afraid of the priests, the landlords, the moneylenders, kidnappers, wild people, robbers, and most of all the evil spirits, devils, and angry gods and goddesses." Of over 4,000 village people in India who were asked to tell what Christ Jesus had done for them 70 per cent included in their reply such a statement as, "He took fear out of me."

In Sarawak, Burma, rural Korea, Africa, and Latin America, we found deliverance from fear mentioned nearly always by people who were bearing public witness to their experience of Christ. "I was always afraid, now I'm never afraid," said one African man. "I was afraid of God, afraid of the devil, afraid of the evil spirits, afraid of the soldiers, afraid of the police, afraid of my creditors, and afraid of the chief," said another African man. A woman said: "I was afraid of my husband and my sons, and even of the pastor and missionary who came to our village, but now I know God is my helper, Jesus my Savior, and the Holy Spirit my guide and teacher. I am not at all afraid now." A very strong impression is made upon tribal people when they meet a happy, healthy, active Christian and find out that he does not observe the taboos they have been taught are necessary to their safety.

An Iban woman told of the surprise she and her husband felt when they became acquainted with a Chinese Christian merchant and learned that he paid no attention to the spirits that had kept them in perpetual panic. "We asked how he kept the evil spirits from destroying him and his family, and he replied, 'I don't do anything; Jesus saves me from the evil spirits and from my sins!' We thought Jesus was a Chinese god. But he told us Jesus was neither a Chinese, nor an Iban, but is ready to protect and save all who believe in him."

There are vast numbers in the world still living in fear. And they are not all in tribal communities. Some live in palatial houses and move in select circles. Some hold college degrees and can talk learnedly on many subjects. But whether in primitive tribes or in families of wealth and social privilege, all who live in fear are people who have never learned the facts about God's love or have refused his call to love and serve him and their fellowmen. In the abundant life that Jesus offers to all who truly believe in him and do the works that he did, there is no room or reason for fear. As churches grow in strength and number fear diminishes. And as individuals and groups freed from fear bear witness to Christ as their Deliverer multitudes turn to the Lord in search of this precious freedom.

IV

How Protestant Churches Obstruct and Counteract Communism

No nation in which Protestant churches wield large influence has come under Communist domination, and today Communism is held in check in every such country. This is no accident or coincidence. The Protestant conscience firmly rejects all forms of totalitarian rule in church and state and demands both political and religious liberty.

Protestant Christians find in the Old and New Testaments, which they read and urge others to read, the Word of God. Exercising the right of interpreting it without totalitarian direction, they acquire the ancient prophets' scorn of tyranny and the apostles' concern for the rule of justice and love. Modern democracy is an outgrowth of Protestant Christianity, and wherever Protestantism is firmly established democracy flourishes. Where the judgment of people is so suspect that they are not encouraged to study the Scriptures and to interpret them, there is natural hesitation about democracy in political life. Wherever Roman Catholicism dominates, autocracy flourishes. How can it be otherwise when that church is itself under autocratic control?

Communism has been called a Christian heresy. Such warrant as there may be for this remark is the recognition of two facts: (a) The professed social concern and idealism of Communist theory had its origin in Christ's teaching; and (b) the materialistic philosophy, militant atheism, and ruthless behavior that dominate Communist practices are gross departures from Christian standards. Perhaps Communism could not have arisen from paganism or any religion outside the stream of Judeo-Christian concern for social justice or have evolved in its present form and character without heretical denial of basic Christian teaching.

Failure by the church in Russia to fulfill the obligations of discipleship undoubtedly contributed to the resentments that Communists have exploited to acquire and retain power. Jesus identified himself with needy people—the hungry, the sick, and the oppressed. To feed a hungry man would be to feed him, to visit a prisoner in jail would be to visit him. He repeatedly told his disciples to heal the sick, cleanse the leper, and open the eyes of the blind. He even made compliance with that order the test of discipleship. "He who believes in me will also do the works that I do." But the church in Russia in the era of the Czars was not with Christ on the side of the oppressed, the sick, and the handicapped, as often as it was on the side of the exploiters of the needy. Oppressive rulers captured control of the church and while professing to be Christian demonstrated their lack of belief by indifference to, if not contempt for, the needy.

By a strange confusion of thought we hear voices raised today to denounce with equal force both Communists and those disciples of Jesus who are proving their belief in him by siding with needy people against their oppressors. The Portuguese government in Angola, after oppressing the people most cruelly for generations, murdered them by the thousands in 1961 for daring

63

to ask for liberty and justice, and are denouncing their critics everywhere as Communists and Communist sympathizers.

Certain confused theological obscurantists have joined misguided devotees of ecclesiastical totalitarianism and panic-stricken manipulators of public opinion in denouncing eminent Protestant clergymen as pro-Communist. G. Bromley Oxnam, bishop of The Methodist Church, author of notable denunciations of Communism, and hard-hitting critic of wrongdoing in business, politics, and racial relations, has been most unjustly attacked. E. Stanley Jones, dedicated world evangelist and one of the most beloved and most effective of missionaries, has been virulently denounced. These men are, and have been consistently, anti-Communist and are among the leaders in the effort to make the church like Christ in concern for the needy of the earth. How anyone could hope to harm Communism by representing these men as Communist sympathizers is hard to understand!

Anything that silences the voice of the prophets and makes disciples of Jesus afraid to teach, preach, and practice the gospel of Christ is a positive aid to the Communist conspirators. The gospel of Jesus is decidedly social in its message and implications. Take from his life and teaching social elements—God's love for man, man's duty to God and his fellowmen, sin's tragic effects or Jesus' call for penitence and promise of pardon and new life—and what is left? Not the full gospel certainly! Only the full gospel gives man enough understanding and strength to reject and repel the shrewd men who come preaching class war and seizure and redistribution of wealth, and promising to end oppression and produce a paradise for all except those whom they choose to name "enemies of the people."

Communism denounces all religions as evil. Some Christians counter by defending all religions as good. The simple fact is that all over the world people are found in considerable number who, on the basis of their own experience and observations, tend to agree with the Communists on this point. Millions of others also would agree had they not learned from the work of Christian missions that religion often is a helpful influence. A young Brahman in India said to the writer: "I abhor the wrongs practiced by Hinduism against the Untouchables. I equally abhor the wrongs done by Islam during its long misrule in India. But I can't accept the Communist denunciation of all religion because Christian missions have done and are doing so much good in my country and all over the world."

Another Brahman who has been converted to Christ testifies as follows: "When the partition of India took place I was in an area of The Punjab that was made a part of Western Pakistan. Before I could depart for my home across the border Moslems began killing Hindus. Christian friends hid me in their home by day and at night guided me toward the border and hid me in the home of other Christians. During the fourth night of travel, always in danger, I got into India. All the time I was fleeing I kept thinking Islam is a bad religion. Hinduism is better. My people won't be killing Moslems as Moslems are killing Hindus. But when I crossed over the border I found that Hinduism was as bad as Islam. Hindus were killing Moslems in India exactly as Moslems were killing Hindus in Pakistan. I began to hate religion.

"But fortunately I remembered how Christians had risked their lives to save me from the Moslems. Then I found that other Christians had actually died trying to save Moslems in

65

India. Communism was teaching us to kill capitalists. I decided that instead of denouncing all religion I should adopt the religion that taught that God is love and that all men should love one another. Now I am happy and wish that all people might love God as we Christians are taught to do."

Many African villagers resent the way that pagan religions have contributed to the manifold miseries in which they and their people have lived. Eager to rise above the cultural and economic ceilings of their traditional life they find themselves blocked and frustrated by the religious beliefs and practices of their people. If they did not know something of Christianity they would turn eagerly to Communism. Where Christian missions have as yet not been established or have been started but have been ineffectual, Communism has made rapid progress. Where missions have worked with wisdom and zeal, adjusting to the needs of the people and producing a vigorous church, Communism has made little headway.

Likewise primitive animists in Assam and Borneo emerging from savage intertribal warfare are turning with joyful relief to the Christian church. They recognize the responsibility of their former religion for many of the miseries that have afflicted them. Many in both countries say quite frankly that if they had to choose between religion as their fathers knew and practiced it and Communism they would choose Communism, but because they know Christ as presented in Christian missions, they are on his side against Communism.

An influential Iban in Sarawak said: "I learned about Communism and Christianity at about the same time, and at first I liked Communism more than Christianity, because I thought it was better to get rid of religion rather than to improve it. But

I heard of how Communists killed people who stood in their way and I knew we didn't need any more killing. We have had too much of that. So I preferred Christianity and how grateful I am!"

When Communism swept to power in China many missionaries escaped by way of India. Knowing the conditions that had prevailed before a network of Christian missions was spread across India, and not realizing how Christian group movements of the underprivileged, aided by Christian schools and hospitals, had forced a reconstruction of religious thinking, social ideals, and political practice, these missionaries expected Communism to sweep across India in a few weeks or months. Indian Christians and their missionary colleagues told these friends from China that India certainly would not go Communist soon and probably would never do so, if the democratic aspirations and endeavors of India received reasonable international support.

Had certain tragic social evils that developed in India during the long centuries of missionary disobedience in the church continued until the arrival of Communism in strength, India would have welcomed its crusade of antireligion. Female infanticide; suttee (the custom of a Hindu widow being cremated on the funeral pyre of her husband); child marriage; exclusion of approximately 20 per cent of the people from temple, school, and courtroom; their banishment from the village to segregated suburbs; their restriction to the lowliest and least remunerative forms of employment; and, worst of all, their being taught to despise themselves were not expressions of good religion. It is to the advantage of the church in its worldwide struggle with Communism that Hinduism had been radically reconstructed, under the impact of Christian missions and in deference to world opinion, before that ruthless enemy began a major effort to conquer India.

Another great advantage comes from the presence of twelve to fifteen million professing Christians, thoroughly Indian in culture and loyalty. These believers in Christ are widely scattered in all parts of the country and are spreading the leaven of the gospel with accelerating rapidity. They are not as deeply Christian as the teachings of Jesus call for, but unfortunately that is generally true of church members everywhere. India's Christians compare favorably with those of any other country, the best with the best, the average with the average. The ability to perceive spiritual truth and to respond to it, like other abilities of heart and mind, seems to be equitably distributed among nations and races.

In Malaya too the Christian church and the effect of its witness, which have penetrated every area of the multiracial, multicreedal nation, have produced determined resistance to Communism. Some years ago the Reds controlled many jungle regions and pessimistic newspaper correspondents were prophesying early victory for their armies throughout the Southeast Asian Peninsula and the adjacent Indonesian Archipelago. Now conditions are stabilized and Communist influence is weak. Military action was not the sole, or even the chief reason, for the failure of those gloomy predictions and the growth of non-Communist sentiment. Christian missions have shown the better way.

When Communist armies from North Korea swept deep into the South Korean Republic in a carefully planned surprise attack, their first objective in many towns and villages was the destruction of the Protestant church and its ministerial and lay leaders. They left no room for doubt that they regarded Protestant Christianity as the foe they needed to fear most. And when United Nations forces drove the Communists back into North Korea they in retreat took with them many of the most influential clergymen and presumably put them to death. At least not one of these men has been seen or heard from since. During all the turmoil and tragedy of the years following the partition and subsequent invasion, the people of the South Korean Republic have been moving Christward. They see as clearly now as the Communists did earlier that Christian discipleship nourishes democracy and its institutions.

Probably it was in Africa, below the Equator, that the Communists, conspiring for world domination, expected their most speedy victory. The pagan masses there had little reason to feel grateful for what their religions had done for them. They were unlikely to reject the promised paradise of communist atheistic materialism in favor of retaining the blessings of their own old religions. What were the contributions of religion to their life? Tribal wars, ritual murder, cannibalism, domestic slavery, the killing of twins and the helpless aged, chronic undernourishment, general illiteracy, the rule of capricious tyrants, and the prevalence of numberless weird and costly superstitions!

Furthermore the longtime experience of Africans with other religions was not encouraging. It had produced many fears and resentments. For more than a thousand years Moslems from North Africa and Arabia had made periodic raids on them, taking their strongest sons and most attractive daughters into slavery. And Europeans, supposed to be Christians, had committed every conceivable crime in dealing with them. That there had come among them both Moslems and Christians who were kind, gentle, and helpful could not altogether overcome their hostile attitude and reactions to the misdeeds of the others.

When Christian missionaries first came down the coast of West Africa to the regions now known as Ghana and Nigeria they were welcomed joyfully. Kings, chiefs, and great numbers of the common people became Christians. There was no hesitation about making a choice. The religion presented by the missionaries was recognized as vastly superior to what they had previously known. But when the missionary was followed by the trader, the slave dealer, and the usurping colonial ruler, the enthusiasm for the white man's religion subsided.

Had Europe been really Christian in dealing with these newly discovered people below the Sahara the whole population would probably have become Christian within a century. It was primarily the slave trade that drove Africa back to paganism. Had Africa's experience with slave dealers who called themselves Christians continued to determine her understanding of Christianity, it is altogether likely that the Communist hopes for a speedy victory would have been quickly realized.

But during the last hundred years Christian missions have established a network of stations all over the subcontinent. Churches, schools, hospitals, and related service projects have given a convincing demonstration of the social values of true religion. In the missionary they have seen the exact opposite of the slave raider, and in the changed life of those of their countrymen who have followed Christ they have seen the promise of a better life for all. To the understanding student of Africa today it is clear that such intelligent and forceful opposition to Communism as exists is evoked by appreciation of Christian missions and especially by the vast, though partial, acceptance of Christian teaching. Communism is strongest where paganism and resentment against the unchristian behavior of oppressors have prepared the people to welcome opposition to religion, and weakest wherever the people have seen in others and developed for themselves the fruits of Christian discipleship.

It should be noted that the pioneer missionaries along the West Africa Coast were Portuguese priests and that they proclaimed in the name of the Vatican that the rightful ruler there was the king of Portugal. King John of Portugal, in exercise of the authority given him by the Pope, sent administrators to rule for him. They instituted high taxation and forced labor, built many large churches and a few monasteries, and undoubtedly did much of value to the people. But alas, the king also gave letters of authority to some of his subjects to take slaves and transport them to markets overseas. The priests were unhappy about this development and insisted that no baptized persons be made slaves. Unfortunately they did not oppose slavery as such.

A little later a Catholic bishop set up an altar on the shore and blessed the slave ships. Baptized Christians became involved in the traffic, accompanying the slave raiders as they went into the interior and brought their victims in chains. Priests who did not even know the language of the captives were sent under deck on the ships to baptize them so that "if the ships sink only their bodies will be lost, while their souls will be saved." What a caricature of baptism!

That longtime close association of the Portuguese government with the slave traffic on one side and its continuing connection with the Roman Catholic Church on the other has increased the difficulty of presenting Christ to Africans as Savior and their

71

faithful Friend and the church as his agency for service. The fact that the Portuguese authorities even now are suppressing liberty and imposing foreign rule with cruel severity is obstructing the evangel and aiding Communism immensely. The Communist crimes against Hungarian patriots were not worse than the Portuguese crimes today against the people of Angola!

In visits to Kenya, Mozambique, Northern and Southern Rhodesia, the Union of South Africa, the Congo, and Ghana the writer has talked with hundreds of Africans of various races, languages, and conditions, including pagans, Christians, and Moslems. He has never heard one pagan express appreciation for the religion of his fathers. He found that many pagans who have established no contact with the church try to give the impression when meeting strangers that they are Christians. The question, "In what religion do you believe?" addressed to over one hundred persons known by prior or later inquiry to be pagans, brought the answer in a large majority of cases, "The Christian religion." Many added, "Of course." It seems clear that the old paganisms cannot henceforth hold either the mind or heart of any African group for long.

In Latin America, too, Communism makes effective use of its antagonism to religion. It is significant that Castro in trying to fasten Communism upon Cuba has attacked the Roman Catholic Church, and that he and his associates are almost all former Roman Catholics. Practicing Protestants, by their direct access to the Bible and by their faith in the priesthood of the believer and the witness of the Holy Spirit to their spirits, develop an inner strength which protects them against Communist attacks. Undoubtedly the practicing Roman Catholic also has a source of strength. The Christian, who is only nominal in his profession, whatever his denominational affiliation or background may be, is a more likely victim of Communist duplicity than the actively practicing Christian, be he Protestant and Evangelical, or Catholic and Sacerdotal.

In Bolivia, where Spanish invaders treacherously murdered the Inca and enslaved the races that comprised his great empire, the people were compelled to become Roman Catholics. But the church turned from the work given it by the Lord and became the ally and agent of the state in depriving the people of knowledge of their past achievements, destroying their culture, teaching them to despise their past, and holding them for generations in ignorance and dire poverty. A few who married Spaniards were allowed to rise a little above the masses. And a still smaller number were granted special favors or made owners of vast landed estates and rich mines and officers of the state or church. Many of the Bolivian priests have brought little honor to God or to their church. While they are not permitted to marry, a high proportion of them father children outside of marriage. Many are such heavy drinkers that they are often unable for weeks at a time to carry out their allotted priestly duties. The laboring classes, unable to bear their troubles in patience, have a smoldering resentment against the Catholic Church and are easily induced by agitators, Communist or non-Communist, to oppose it as the ally of their oppressors.

At present in this Andean republic, Protestant churches are growing rapidly. A grandson of a Catholic priest said to the writer: "The only way to save Bolivia and the other Andean countries from Communism is to let them see better religion in action. This is the reason the Catholic hierarchy is importing priests from North America and Europe. But they are too late

73

to save Bolivia from Communism by changing the Catholic Church here. Many prefer, as I and my family do, to accept the uncorrupted evangelical faith as we find it in the Bible." And a Roman Catholic with whom the writer talked said: "We of the laboring classes have been brought up as Catholics and it is hard for us to become something else. But we all know the sympathies of the Catholic Church have been with our oppressors, and we know that unless that changes the country will become either Communist or Protestant. It will not remain Roman Catholic in the historic sense of Catholicism in this part of the world."

At the beginning of the twentieth century there were said to be only 175,000 Evangelical Christians in Brazil. In 1960 the number was reported to be about 6,000,000. And the elements that provide the best protection against Communism in Brazil are these Protestants and the oriental immigrants. These latter do not share the grievances of their impoverished, and often illiterate, neighbors against Roman Catholicism, but they do witness what it does to their fellow Brazilians. An immigrant from Communist North Korea, after two years in Brazil, said: "I became a Protestant in Korea and had to flee because of the Communists. And if the Communists get here soon most of my neighbors will join them because they see so little that is good in religion. They do not believe in Catholicism but in spiritism. I'm trying to bring them to a saving faith in Jesus. If Brazil develops real Christian faith before the Communists can gain control we'll have a wonderful country." One of the largest and most rapidly growing congregations in the world today is in Sao Paulo, Brazil. It is associated with the Assemblies of God, a very Protestant church. The usual Sunday evening attendance is said to exceed twelve thousand. This very commodious structure was erected with funds almost all given by Brazilian members of the congregation.

Other illustrations come out of Communist China and Tibet. The writer has talked with approximately a hundred refugees from those disturbed lands. Asking them what effect the Communist campaign against religion was having, the reply of Christians and non-Christians alike very often included sentiments like the following: "The Communists make much of the claim that those who were formerly in power, both under the Manchus and the Kuomintang, made use of religion to help repress and control the poor. They argue that religion is always on the side of the people in power, no matter how evil they may be. Most Buddhists who have not known Christian missions agree with them. The Christians know better. They and the minority of Buddhists who have had personal contacts with the church know that Chinese Christians are good neighbors and useful citizens and that Christian missions in pre-Communist days helped the common people and the nation in every way. Christians have an inner strength the Communists don't understand. They are standing up well under the Communist attack. But Buddhism is disintegrating. When eventually the Communists are overthrown these people will turn to Christ by hundreds of thousands."

Buddhist refugees from Tibet are very critical of Buddhism. One of them said: "We came to India, and Christian people whom we had not known before have shown us what religion ought to be. We wish there were Christians in Tibet." A forward-looking Chinese Christian remarked: "Communism in China will fail in time. It is too negative to live long. The people are turning to Communism against their bad old religion but religious longings remain with them. When liberty returns, the people will not revive Buddhism, but will turn to the religion that works."

In India a number of former Communists have been converted. They speak of the ease with which many people are turned against religion. "My Hindu religion meant nothing to me," one of these converts said. "In fact, it seemed a handicap to my country and to me. I knew the priests to be parasites. We had to support them but we could not respect them. So when the Communists told me that religion must be destroyed in order to free the common people I agreed with them quickly."

Another said: "My ancestors were high-caste Hindus. They became Moslems when the Moguls ruled over India. When I was a baby, my parents and thousands of others returned to Hinduism. They were not received with kindness as promised. Again they became Moslems. I was educated in Moslem schools. But I decided that we would be better off with no religion. So did many of our ablest young men. One of my close relatives became a top leader in the Communist Party. I too joined that party. But as I was being trained for responsibility in it I learned that I was expected to lie, steal, and perhaps even to murder for the sake of the party.

"It was then that I asked if there was not one good religion which I could accept and believe and practice. I got a Bible and began studying Christianity. My wife, however, would not consider becoming a Christian. But some months later she became very ill and entered a mission hospital. The kindness of the lady doctors and nurses won her completely. When she came home she said to me: 'Now I am ready to become a Christian. This

76

religion is true. God is in it. These people in the hospital know him.' A few weeks later we confessed Christian faith and were baptized. Now most of our relatives are Christians. Our children also are happy in Christ."

This same convert from Communism wrote me recently: "There are only two choices for thinking people in India today. One, atheism, which leads directly to Communism; the other, theism, which leads to Christ. Christ is the Lord of the future. This I know because Christ has met my needs and my needs are the basic needs of people everywhere. I formerly told people how bad religions are. I now tell them how wonderful Christ Jesus is, how happy he has made me, and how changed I am. I tell them, too, how changed my wife is since Christ came into her life. Then, if they come home with me as they do once in awhile, she confirms what I have said."

A Sikh who has not yet been baptized expressed himself thus: "My community is greatly disappointed. Ninety per cent of our people have lost faith in our religion which has no value to keep it alive in these new times. The Gurus [founders-teachers of Sikhism] saw that Hinduism was wrong and they quit it. Needing a new religion, they took some Hindu beliefs and some Moslem teachings and mixed with them a few improved ideas and produced Sikhism. But they were men like us, good men perhaps, and patriots, but there was not among them a man such as Jesus was. We want to know God and we have faith that we can know him in Jesus Christ. It seems to me that only by accepting Jesus can our young people be saved from Communism."

Another young Sikh, a college professor, has been converted and is now doing advanced study in the United States. He too

77

feels that the best protection against atheistic, ruthless Communism is the preaching and practice of the gospel of Jesus Christ. "The Christian church has the answer to Communism because it has the answer to sin and human need," is his way of putting it.

Often churches are able to stop Communism where governments and armies are unable to do so. Growing churches, rich in knowledge of the Word of God and eager to obey the Savior's command to disciple the nations, present a formidable obstruction to all threats to human welfare. Where such churches are assisted by wise and devoted missionaries they purify oppressive ancient religions and set forth and practice a way of life of the greatest value to everyone in the nation. When a network of congregations spreads over a population bringing to multitudes the abundant and eternal life promised by the Savior, something of the greatest value happens to the nation. And when succeeding generations are reared in the prophets' scorn for tyranny and the apostles' concern for justice and mercy, the best and the only certain and enduring barrier against Communism is erected.

V

Preaching Imperative but Not Sufficient

Preaching is a vital function of the Christian ministry. It was central in the ministry of Jesus. "No man ever spoke like this man!" said officers who heard him. Everything else Jesus did was closely related to his preaching. Likewise our Lord made preparations for preaching central in his training of the twelve. Except for the man of tragedy who betrayed him, all of those chosen men whom Jesus trained became fervent and successful preachers. When Saul the persecutor was converted and transformed into Paul the apostle, he too became a zealous preacher, both convinced and convincing.

Peter and his companions, after the open-air commissioning service conducted by their risen Lord atop a mountain in Galilee and their return to the crowded city of Jerusalem for their upper-room experience of Pentecost, preached with holy boldness and authority. People began to believe and repent and receive new life. Word spread rapidly through the city as it had done wherever and whenever Jesus came preaching. When opposition developed and rulers and elders and scribes questioned their authority, the apostles were not frightened. When they were commanded to speak no more in the name of Jesus, Peter and all the apostles answered, "We must obey God rather than man." New converts became zealous lay preachers. No authority of Israel or of Rome could make them desist. When the church was laid waste, its members being dragged to prison, refugees went everywhere preaching.

While Peter and his associates and the new apostle Paul, did many things for Christ's sake and the gospel's, they never made preaching secondary. The program for the whole of their lives —every day of it—was woven around the preaching of the gospel. Paul wrote to Timothy—his son in the faith—"I was ordained a preacher" (K.J.V.). In his letter to the Romans, he expounds the need for preaching: "How are men to call upon him in whom they have not believed? . . . And how are they to hear without a preacher? . . . Faith comes from what is heard, and what is heard comes by the preaching of Christ." And to the Corinthians he wrote: "Necessity is laid upon me. Woe to me if I do not preach the gospel."

Occasionally an ineffective preacher or an unresponsive layman calls for a suspension of preaching. Usually such calls are linked with the suggestion that deeds not words are needed. But good deeds can no more make preaching unnecessary than hard work can eliminate the need for food. As the physical energy the family requires for the day's task is provided by the food the housewife serves, so the spiritual strength necessary for the work of the church is provided by the Word of God which the preacher ministers. It is the Word, the Truth of God, that provides strength. It may be received from the pulpit or through the press or by the witness of friend or neighbor or through meditation, even as food for the needs of the body is prepared, and may be taken in many different forms and by differing methods.

Preaching of some sort has been a feature of nearly all religions and even of most organized or articulate opposition to religion. In India many schools of Hindu thought are represented by wandering preachers who recite from ancient poetic or prose writings, extolling gods and goddesses and heroes and heroines of bygone days. They call for loyalty to the customs of clan or caste and warn against the acceptance of "evil modern ideas." Throughout Moslem countries and wherever large groups of Moslems live near non-Moslems, lay preachers of Islam abound. In Kashmir, Eastern Pakistan, and parts of Africa these lay preachers have been the most successful propagandists of that iconoclastic faith. Communism is making effective use of the power of the wandering preacher. Probably the most fervent preaching millions in Asia and Africa have heard in recent years has been done by agents of Communism preaching the "gospel" of Karl Marx, the virtue of hating the capitalist, and the infallibility of the Communist system.

Preaching is not always verbal. The daily life of a dedicated Christian who is weak in speech may preach the gospel more effectively than the most powerful master of pulpit eloquence. And no speech is long fully effective that does not have the support of daily life. Every person needs both to hear the gospel preached attractively from the pulpit and to see it preached convincingly in varied life situations by the behavior of true believers.

Across today's world are many who have heard the gospel well preached from the pulpit but not so well presented within their homes or in the lives of their acquaintances. And there are also many in Asia and in Africa who have never heard a formal sermon preached from a pulpit, yet have come to know and

81

believe the gospel as it has been preached in the conversation and behavior of relatives and friends. Many have read not only the life of Christians but the inspired writings from the Book of Books. The church grows most rapidly and most soundly when the man in the pulpit and the man on the street and the friend next door say the same thing in word and behavior as is read in the Gospels of Matthew, Mark, Luke, and John.

The Christian gospel is a body of affirmations and not a system of denials. Jesus affirmed that God is a loving Father, that he forgives the sins of the penitent, that the kingdom of heaven is at hand, and belongs to the poor in spirit and to those who are persecuted for righteousness' sake, that the meek shall inherit the earth, that the merciful shall obtain mercy, that he and the Eternal Father are one, that whosoever believes in him shall not perish but have eternal life, and that he was sent into the world that the world through him might be saved. It is essential that those affirmations be accepted and be made our own. No man has ever been saved from sin by his denials but many have been saved by their affirmations. Faith is affirmative, so is hope, so is love. Paul says we are justified by faith. Elsewhere he says we are saved by hope. Our denials may have real value; they may save us from serious mistakes, but they cannot make us disciples of Jesus or save us from our sins. These affirmations of Christian faith provide the dynamic power needed for church growth everywhere. Our denials make use of power and may eventually exhaust our power resources, but our affirmations generate power.

This writer learned the hard way the danger involved in presenting Christ and Christianity in negative terms. A group of oppressed leather-workers asked him to visit their village and tell them of Christ, explaining that some of their relatives and fellow sufferers as Hindu Untouchables had become Christians and were advising them to do the same. He agreed to come and on the appointed day arrived to find some sixty men and women gathered to hear him. He spoke for more than an hour, entirely in negative terms. Disciples of Jesus should not worship idols, should not drink alcoholic liquors, should not gamble, should not eat the flesh of animals that had died of old age or disease. The speech dealt with harmful practices of the leather-workers of the area. It gave good advice but it was not the gospel.

When the speech was finished a Hindu religious professional, who had been serving as a kind of visiting spiritual adviser to the community, asked if he might speak and obtaining permission, said: "If this missionary has spoken correctly, the Christian religion is better than I had thought. He said, 'Don't drink alcoholic liquors.' I thought all Christians drank regularly. In Calcutta I have seen many Europeans who appeared to drink alcohol everyday. He said, 'Don't gamble.' In Calcutta the Christians have a race track and gamble on every race. He said, 'Don't eat the flesh of animals that have died of old age or disease.' Which of these things did I ever tell you to do? I know you worship idols. I don't object to idol worship, but I don't tell you to do it. Did I ever tell you to drink alcohol or gamble or eat the flesh he forbade you to eat? No, I go farther than he does. If you must eat flesh, it is better to eat without having to kill. Does he prefer that you kill God's creatures to get food? I tell you not to eat any flesh. I also tell you not to eat tomatoes or beets because they are red like blood. I tell you not to eat eggplants because they look like eggs." (The small ones with which they were acquainted did look somewhat like eggs.)

The writer had made a tragic blunder. He had failed completely to present Christ and the gospel to those inquiring needy people. How disappointed they must have been! What sorrow there must have been in heaven over a wasted opportunity! Two years and two months later after many visits and much work by other disciples of Jesus, the writer was granted the privilege of baptizing nearly the entire company of those leather-workers and of receiving them into the fellowship of Christ's disciples. From the experience he learned that Christians dare not reduce the gospel to a body of denials. The church of Christ cannot compete with Hinduism, Buddhism, or even many animistic religions in denials and prohibitions, but no man-made religion can compete with the gospel of Christ in the richness and the power and the glory of its affirmations about God and man and life.

In an African state the writer found denials so overemphasized that many church members seemed to know very little about the gospel. "What makes a man a Christian?" he asked a leading layman.

"He must have only one wife and she must not work in the tobacco fields," was the answer given.

"Are you a Christian?" another was asked.

"Yes," he replied, "I do not drink, smoke, gamble, have a fetish, or beat my wife."

"But what you don't do or don't have does not make you a Christian, you know!" the writer responded. Both the man being questioned and the interpreter seemed to be troubled by this line of inquiry and comment.

A fact that emerges in every study of church growth is the decisive importance of nonprofessional lay preaching and witness.

Non-Christians usually pay the strictest attention to the life of the convert whom they knew before his conversion and are quick to recognize whether the evidence of his changed life supports the claims made that Christ saves from sin. Non-Christian neighbors of the new convert are often very generous in their judgments of him and of the effect of his conversion upon his way of life. They often appraise the change in him more highly than do missionaries and pastors. Asked to explain this fact one generous appraiser said, "The pastor compares the new man with what he wants him to be and is disappointed. We compare him with what he formerly was and are pleased."

In one area in Southern India two missions had publicly preached with impressive zeal and persistence in nearly every village, thereby influencing public opinion and ethics but had not, so far as was known, won anyone to public confession of Christian faith. But both missions established contacts with groups of Untouchables who could not be reached by preaching in the village squares, for they were compelled to live outside the village in segregated quarters. Some of those Untouchables were converted and of the converts a number became zealous unpaid evangelists. At first evangelism through these lay witnesses followed caste lines. But in time the influence of the changed lives of converts, aided undoubtedly by the public preaching within the villages, broke over caste lines. In the churches that have been established through the two missions, members from a number of caste origins now worship in a rich and understanding fellowship.

A detailed study of more than seven hundred families in those churches revealed that testimony of laymen, by word and life, was the most potent influence in their conversion. One man

85

said: "I knew that some people had become Christians but always thought, 'That's not for me,' until the day when in the marketplace a relative talked me into visiting him and going with him to church. When I was in his home we talked for hours. He was so happy as a Christian that I decided that I could not do without what he had found. So I became a Christian. And now all my relatives and neighbors formerly of the Mala caste are Christians."

Now within that section of South India strong movements toward Christian faith and discipleship are developing. They are by no means confined to the original castes within which the earliest movements took place, but in some localities have become community movements uniting a number of caste groups in a common quest for satisfying religious experience. These movements could not have been started without strong, convincing, and persuasive preaching both in words of power and in the witness of life, by missionaries from abroad, by pastors of the area knowing the life and language of the people, and by laymen with a broad community of interest with those to whom they communicated their joyous discoveries.

The evangelists Matthew, Mark, Luke, and John all present Jesus as primarily a preacher but never only as a preacher. Matthew for example says: "He went about all Galilee, teaching . . . and preaching . . . and healing every disease and every infirmity among the people." He clearly did not regard preaching as sufficient. He preached with authority, the best possible, and did it supremely well. Yet he had to confirm what he preached and seems to have made few converts by preaching alone.

John the Baptist, who had proclaimed Jesus as the Messiah,

86

became discouraged and uncertain when in prison and sent his disciples to ask whether Jesus was, in truth, the Messiah. Jesus replied, "Go and tell John what you have seen and heard: the blind receive their sight, the lame walk, lepers are cleansed, and the deaf hear, the dead are raised up, the poor have good news preached to them." Perhaps neither his words nor his works by themselves would have convinced John and put his mind and heart at rest. Together they gave John in prison the satisfying answer that fortified him for the martyrdom that awaited him.

When a poor paralytic was brought to Jesus and he, seeing the man's deeper need, first addressed himself to it saying, "Man, your sins are forgiven you," the Pharisees were disturbed. To them Jesus offered, as proof of his power to forgive sins, his healing of the man. " 'That you may know that the Son of man has authority on earth to forgive sins'—he said to the man who was paralyzed—'. . . Rise, take up your bed and go home.' " Whether this convinced the Pharisees we do not know, but the crowds looking on "glorified God and were filled with awe." Unlike some of his modern ministers, Jesus did not demand acceptance of his claims just because he made them. Having called upon people to love God with their minds, he expected them to use their minds in considering him, his words, and his works, and he gave abundant reasons for the faith he asked them to exercise. These reasons convinced the disciples. Peter said: "You have the words of eternal life; and we have believed, and have come to know, that you are the Holy One of God." Nicodemus saw his works proving his words true, "We know that you are a teacher come from God; for no one can do these signs that you do, unless God is with him." Repeatedly those whom he healed and those who saw the healing take place recognized it as evi-

87

dence of God's response to Jesus. They "gave praise to God."

This confirmation of the preaching of Jesus by his mighty works was twofold. His works showed that he loved people, despite their sins and sicknesses, and that he was able to bring the power of God to bear upon their needs and to meet those needs fully. When Jesus preached that God is love, and acts always as the Heavenly Father and that he and the Father are one, so that in him they saw the Father, he had to be and to demonstrate love. Had he not served people in love how could his preaching have been regarded as true! And again had his love been displayed unmistakably but no healing been brought to the sick and blind and leprous, how could they have believed that he was one with the omnipotent God? He did not send his chosen twelve out to preach until he had first shown them the massive misery about them in their own Galilean villages, called them to pray for the sufferers, and given them the authority to heal.

Had these men, in training to be apostles, closed their minds to the sufferings of the people or for any reason decided to limit their responsibility to preaching a sermon every sabbath morning there would be no Christian church today.

A sad commentary on the fallibility of the human mind, even when devoted to God, is the announcement made by a few enthusiastic missionary organizations that they use all their funds in "preaching the gospel." Even in the midst of preaching in a synagogue, Jesus stopped to heal a sick man. And he never, as far as the record goes, appointed anyone to do nothing but preach.

Teaching, preaching, and healing—inseparable in the ministry of Jesus—are projected in twentieth-century discipleship as school, church, and hospital. In presenting Christ to people who live in a predominantly non-Christian culture, where education and medical service have not been and are not otherwise available, these linked endeavors are most necessary. Where the church is at the center in a well-integrated service of preaching, teaching, and healing, the best results are obtained. The Christian who educates without imparting faith in the Christ or who heals the body without revealing Christ as Lord and Savior falls short in missionary obedience and betrays the Gospels.

There were critics of the healing ministry of Jesus. The Pharisees, motivated perhaps in part by objection to his theology and in part by fear of the effect of his growing popularity upon their standing in the community, resented his healing. Sometimes they belittled it. They even attributed it to a suspected alliance with unseen evil forces. "He casts out demons by the prince of demons." In like manner the healing ministry of the church today is criticized. "The church has no right to make converts by healing the sick. They are taking advantage of ill people to subvert their religion. Let them convert well people whose minds are not weakened so that they will give up their religion to escape from their misery." Thus spoke a Hindu extremist, attacking Christian missions.

In response to a political agitation, the government of one Indian state, Bombay, some years ago started to treat patients who were afflicted with leprosy in their hospitals. They did so because agitators claimed that sufferers from leprosy were becoming Christians under the mistaken belief that only Christian missionaries could cure leprosy. These agitators demanded that the government start hospitals and staff them with non-Christians, so that leprosy patients, their relatives, and the public might know that religion makes no difference in healing disease. But after fifteen or twenty years the government of Bombay state asked Christian missionary organizations to take over the hospitals. The government promised to continue providing the funds as needed. The official letter on the subject said: "We find that for the successful treatment of leprosy a missionary spirit is essential. Government doctors and nurses object to being assigned to this work."

Dr. Manohar Masih, a dedicated Indian Christian leprologist, asked for ordination and qualified for it by extended study, because he felt that medicines and diet could be reinforced powerfully by a ministry of the Word and the Sacraments. "Prayer, praise, and fellowship are powerful therapeutic forces in curing leprosy," Dr. Masih likes to say. This sincere disciple of Jesus makes it clear to all his patients that the help he gives them is in no way dependent on their confessing Christian faith, but he would like them to know Jesus Christ and make him their Lord. The joy of many of Dr. Masih's once-hopeless patients as they bear witness for Christ and his servants is contagious. It has mystified Hindus who have come in a mood of hostility and have stayed to admire and appreciate. Despite the critics, the cleansing of lepers continues to prove the gospel to many people and the church grows thereby. A fervent African Christian said: "I never believed the gospel to be true and never overcame my dislike for white people until I saw a British missionary tenderly caring for Africans who were smitten with leprosy. I felt that white people don't naturally love black people and that no one, white or black, likes to look at one whose face is made hideous by leprosy, so I knew that God was with that white man. Now I too love God and the hatred I felt for white people has been taken out of my heart—entirely."

Experience of missions has established two facts firmly. When the love of God is to be expressed in the healing ministry, care must be taken to guard against any tendency to serve Christians preferentially. As Jesus said in the Sermon on the Mount, God "sends rain upon the just and on the unjust." Non-Christians are adversely affected when Christians preach God's love for all mankind but help sick Christians rather than sick non-Christians. Often non-Christians suspect their chances of being served faithfully in a Christian hospital are increased if they profess Christian faith or show interest in Christianity.

In the second place converts should become as soon as possible participants in the healing ministry. Their spiritual well-being demands that they cease as soon as possible to be beneficiaries only of that ministry. As in preaching the gospel and in teaching in Christian schools the largest success is not attainable until local Christians share in healing the sick. By all means local Christians must prove the truth of the gospel. Many people concede that the gospel is true for the missionary and his kind of people before they believe that it is true for them and for others in their society.

The interpretation of the duty of Christians to heal the sick as being restricted to so-called spiritual healing is a tragic mistake. God is the only Healer. All healing in human experience is by his will and mercy. Jesus never said a word against physicians or the use of medicines. His devoted disciple, Luke, was a professional medical man. A dedicated physician or surgeon, who has spent years studying medicine, or a heroic nurse, who devotes her whole life to a healing ministry that demands daily subordi-

91

nation to the judgments of the doctor and a sacrificial income, can certainly express God's love as well as it can be done by the practitioner of spiritual healing. Sympathy with the sick and afflicted and the will to help are the marks of a Christian, not an obscurantist objection to the use of remedies that God has placed within man's reach and man has learned to use by exercising mental abilities that are also God-given.

In the course of forty-six years of service in India the writer knew personally seven missionaries who refused to be vaccinated against smallpox on the ground that its use would indicate a lack of faith in God. All seven of these men and women, despite their devotion, died of smallpox. And they were not the only victims of their lamentable confusion on this issue, for a good many humble Indian Christians were taught by them to take the same attitude and many of them also died of smallpox.

The ministry of Jesus brings preaching, teaching, healing, and personal service to needy people into right relation to one another. No one of these services can produce maximum values if separated from the others. Preaching the gospel of God's love without doing these other things that Jesus did is self-defeating. Doing any one or all of these other things without preaching the gospel may be humanitarian but is not fully Christian. The coming of the Kingdom for which our Lord taught his disciples to pray awaits the development of a world church with a full program built upon the words and works of Jesus.

VI

Yesterday's Best Not Good Enough Today

Today's demands on the church cannot be met with yesterday's religion. That needs to be said until it is firmly fixed in the minds of church members all across the world. Every component part of a Christianity that works needs to be fresh. Faith, hope, love, and the consciousness of the nearness and favor of God must be renewed daily in the life of each Christian to prevent rust, erosion, and conformity to the world. "Be transformed by the renewal of your mind, that you may prove what is the will of God," says the ever-effective Paul. And again says he, "Let your speech always be gracious, seasoned with salt, so that you may know how you ought to answer every one." If renewal is necessary to knowledge of the will of God, and speech must be gracious and interesting to produce the right answers to those outside the church, then it should be clear that we dare not go through these days into the tomorrows with yesterday's religion.

The young people of today cannot meet their obligations as Christians with their parents' religion. They themselves must know God. They themselves must believe in Jesus Christ and accept and practice his teachings. Their generation needs to be more deeply Christian than any prior one has ever been if it is

93

to meet the demands of this decisive time in history. The generation now yielding control to younger folk can hardly deny that it has forfeited much of the opportunity God gave it for furthering his kingdom on earth. The next generation must have more Christian faith and devotion, not just as much.

In every period and within every nation there has developed a tendency to glorify the past. Nostalgic memory is notoriously inaccurate. No matter how bad a situation may be, when change sets in lamentations begin. There are always a few, at least, who are too well adjusted to the prevailing wrongs of their social order to face the prospect of change happily.

Memory is selective. In India since independence, the writer has often heard people, who were eating better than they had eaten in pre-independence days, talk mournfully of the high cost of rice, forgetful of the fact that when rice was cheap they did not have enough money to buy a third of what they needed. Excessive cheerfulness about the past contributes to uneasiness about the future. The voice of the pessimist has never been completely muted anywhere. When middle-aged and elderly pessimists begin deploring the evil ways of the young they usually forget how their elders condemned them when they were young. As their selective memories reconstruct their youth, those were the days of goodness, wisdom, and nobility.

If one had to read and believe all the lamentations that have survived in the world's literature he would probably be depressed beyond the possibility or desire to rise again. But after reading a few dozen assorted selections from different periods and areas, he would begin to understand that man is most prone to error when he listens primarily to his fears and speaks most freely against his juniors. The times which see the most improvement in morals, government, conditions of the poor, and common religious practices are precisely the times when the cries of the pessimists are loudest and most raucous and criticism is most virulent. The Protestant Reformation unleashed a torrent of denunciation. The open-air preaching and fervent hymn singing of the Wesleyan revival, with the determined upsurge of the previously docile and inarticulate lower classes, produced a chorus of full-throated pessimism about the future of the church and the nation.

In all cultures change has generally been decried by the privileged who have been the most articulate elements in the population. The inarticulate masses have often enormously gained by the very changes that were so deplored. The literature of pessimism bridges all chasms between languages and religions.

Even with missions, developments bringing great growth to the church have often been opposed as lamentable. An example is the mass movements of people that have produced three fourths of the strength of the church in India and nine tenths of the church in Burma. A well-meaning and learned, but very mistaken missionary, in the last quarter of the nineteenth century wrote and spoke powerfully against these "mass movements," saying that they would postpone by a thousand years the evangelization of the real India, by which he meant the high-caste Hindus.

We are now in history's first period of universal and all-pervading change. For the first time a world culture is in the making. Inevitably the changes now taking place will deprive many people of cherished privileges. They will transfer political responsibilities from people who regard themselves as well qualified by experience and understanding to people who are inexperienced and not obviously qualified otherwise. The balance of power between races and nations is shifting rapidly. Long professed codes of behavior in economics and politics, and even in war, are being challenged and openly disregarded. Hidden within this world change are possibilities of world catastrophe. These possibilities are stimulating pessimists to utterance, unprecedented in volume and folly. Newspaper correspondents, editors, radio and television commentators, retired army officers, a few oil magnates with more dollars than sense, and even some preachers are vying with one another as prophets of doom and inciters of panic.

The time has come for Christian men and women to declare war on this menacing pessimism. It is an enemy of Christian faith, a terrible deterrent to the growth of the church, and a danger to the welfare of all peoples. Its most direct effect is to strengthen Communism and other enemies of the kingdom of God. Clearly many of those, who have surrendered to this evil force, and are now doing incalculable harm by promoting its spread among others, have no comprehension of its true position in the world. One wealthy man alarmed by the spread of Communism urged that no more money be given to missions in Asia because it was clear to him that the whole of Asia is going Communist within a few years. A correspondent of a widely read American magazine wrote an article saying that the whole of Asia must by now be regarded as within the orbit of Communism and "lost." How any good can proceed from that kind of reckless panic inciting is hard to understand.

In this welter of confusion the Christian is called upon to make a new and deeper dedication of himself to Christ and begin to develop afresh the Christian virtues of faith, hope, and love. Looking at the world's rampaging needs with the insight that comes through faith and love, every Christian should now say, "Lord, I believe," even though he may have to add, in the words of an honest and loving father of old, "Help thou my unbelief." He has no right ever to say, "Lord, I won't believe. Help me to hold firm my unbelief." Throughout the world today the traveler, who looks for it, will discover faith in Jesus Christ but he will find no area that is entirely free from doubt. Possibilities of the greatest good for all mankind abound today, but they can only be realized by an awakened faith and a fresh dedication to the purposes of God. Even the zealous pessimist may be transformed into an agent of God's love and a harbinger of a new era of unprecedented growth and victory for the church.

There is now, as was so often in past crises, a wide and mistaken belief that what is most needed and what the Church should strive for most earnestly is a return to the "old-time religion." By this euphemistic expression is commonly meant the religious beliefs, attitudes, and practices of fifty, seventy-five, a hundred, two hundred, or even five hundred years ago. A little objective study should convince sincere Christians that such return would be disastrous. The church today is far more Christian than it was one, two, three, five, or ten generations or as many centuries ago. A return to the old-time religion would retard church growth and drive from the fellowship its most Christian sections.

If we take as a criterion of the condition of the church its response to the missionary mandate Jesus gave, we see at once that two hundred years ago Protestants were almost completely indifferent and disobedient. Even a hundred years ago most Protestant church members were doing nothing to make dis-

97

ciples of Christ outside of their own countries or nations. While proclaiming faith in the deity of Christ and in the Scriptures, they ignored their missionary obligations as completely as some Christians today ignore the gospel's racial implications. When Christians in Great Britain first became concerned about their missionary obligations they had the greatest difficulty in finding qualified young men and women in England, Scotland, Ireland, or Wales who were willing to accept appointment to distant lands. Consequently many early missionaries supported in Asia by British churches were Germans. When a young man pleaded to send missionaries to Asia an elder reproved him with the classic words, "Sit down, young man. When God wants to save the heathen, he will do so without your help or mine."

The inadequacy of the old-time religion is reflected in the experience of an American businessman who called on the writer in Delhi some years ago. After introducing himself he asked, "Can you explain why Christians in America have not been told about the importance of missions in Asia? I have had two heart attacks. After the first I retired and moved West. A few years later I started a new business. Then came my second attack. The doctors made me retire again and go abroad. For six months I have been in Asia. Here I see forces developing which will likely determine the world's future. The church has done wonders but is working with totally inadequate resources. Why did I have to come here to find this out?" Soon he himself gave the answer. It came out that he had been brought up in a very limited, old-fashioned home that objected to many "new-fangled practices" including allowing "heathen Chinese" to come to "Christian America" and would not give to foreign missions, "because all that money is needed here in our own country." When free from the control of his parents, he turned completely away from Christian profession for a brief time. Then he joined another church and accepted more adequate ideas of Christianity, but strangely clung tenaciously to the anti-foreign-missions attitude of his parents. On the first Sunday of each year for many years he gave twenty dollars to the pastor and said, "Put that into your missionary fund and don't mention foreign missions to me again all year." The old-time religion of his parents had piled up obstacles in the way of his approach to a Christian discipleship adequate for these times.

Another man's experience with old-time religion produced tragic results for him and for those closest to him. He had accepted the religion of his parents, as he understood it. He became a regular attendant at church services and an active participant in the weekly prayer meeting, class meeting, and Sunday school. But his life was compartmentalized. Religion was for the church and the dining room of the home. In the latter it was allowed limited influence. From his business it was rigidly excluded. His business practices were notoriously unethical. He became very rich and very stingy. In his home he was an autocrat. His children were compelled to do his bidding at all times in all matters. His business associates disliked him and his competitors hated him. But he remained in good standing in the church. After his death his widow and all his children turned away from the church. Whatever it was that would make anyone associate this kind of religion with the life and teachings of Jesus Christ is understandable only in the light of man's strange genius for rationalizing the irrational.

The testing of the old-time religion by the church's contact with African slavery provides forceful lessons. Protestants generally disapproved of slavery when the traffic was new. But profits reconciled a minority to the point that they became slave owners and slave dealers. At least one pioneer missionary in Africa resigned in order to engage in the slave trade. Another wrote a defense of the slave traffic on biblical grounds. In America many ministers of old-time religion bought and sold slaves. The southern wife of a Methodist bishop, himself born in the North, owned a slave a few years before the Civil War and the bishop's acquiescence in his wife's ownership contributed substantially to the division of the Methodist Church into two bodies. That division persisted until 1939.

If the church had not become Christian enough to speak with undivided conviction against slavery, it would never have acquired the moral influence it now wields. Enlightened conscience the whole world over is now hostile to slavery. But the evil effects of that sin and of the complicity of Christian people, Protestants and Catholics alike, toward it are still felt throughout the world. They have recently been seen in the disgraceful demonstrations in New Orleans against white parents who had the courage to keep their children in a certain school after Negro children had been admitted to it. They are seen in recent assaults upon Freedom Riders, and in the closing of the schools in a Virginia county because white people in control were determined that their children should not attend classes with Negro children. They are seen in the misbehavior of white racists in the Union of South Africa acting with extraordinary unawareness of how the Christian conscience of people, not related as they are to the situation, rejects and condemns their behavior. These professed Christians confirm a long recognized fact about human behavior, namely that self-deception is very easy and terribly

100

dangerous. On both the North American and African continents these racists are retarding the growth of the church of Christ and helping its Communist and other enemies all over the world.

Another reason the church cannot return to the religion of earlier generations is the tragic weakness of its earlier opposition to war. Today's need is for utter loyalty to the Prince of Peace and uncompromising opposition to war. The church in the past has blessed wars with a shocking frequency. Army commanders with records of shocking brutality against their own troops, committed in the name of discipline, and against opposing forces and civilian populations, committed in the name of patriotism, have been made national heroes by Christian nations, with the implied approval of the church. Prayers have been offered for success in wars of open aggression. A distinguished hymn writer was prominent in the direction of the war by which China was compelled to grant facilities for the sale of opium to her people. He wrote beautifully of the Cross of Christ but laid aside the obligations of the Golden Rule and waged war to further misconceived national interests.

The church today is under the call of God to be more Christian in its attitudes toward war than it has been in many crises of the past. Perhaps the greatest difficulty most Christians now experience in formulating an attitude of unrelenting opposition to war grows out of the influence exercised upon them by Christian participation in past wars. Pessimists to the contrary notwithstanding, the behavior of Christian nations in international affairs is generally on a higher moral level than was the case at any time that might be brought to mind by talk of "the old-time religion." But constant vigilance is required now to keep governments mindful of the need for righteousness in dealing with

101

one another. Because of our involvements in the tensions that place peace in jeopardy, we are in danger of deceiving ourselves about the issues, letting our own hatreds, prejudices, or fears blind us to the religious issues involved.

Other inadequacies in the old-time religion are clearly revealed in the record. Despite the love Jesus showed for children and the instructions he gave about caring for them, the church throughout the Middle Ages and in earlier centuries allowed millions of God's little ones to be mistreated cruelly. Millions in every age of the church's life have grown up without education—religious or secular. Christians with ample resources were content if their own children got limited instruction and did little or nothing to plan educational opportunity for the children of other and poorer families. When the industrial revolution came in Europe, children were often made to work as much as twelve hours a day. The church did not even start Sunday schools until relatively modern times. As late as the eighteenth century children were hanged by consent of the church for stealing a loaf of bread.

Our selective memories have allowed us to forget the terrible neglect of Christian education that put into the pulpit of the established Church of England in the seventeenth century many men who could recite neither the Lord's Prayer nor the Ten Commandments. One Anglican bishop reported asking one of his pastors what is meant by the expression, "The Lord's Prayer," and receiving the answer, "It is a prayer our lord the king has prepared for us to use in public worship." In this matter of caring for children, Christian people in their churches and through their governments have made many improvements. Further improvements are needed now. Yesterday's best in education is not good enough for today's children.

In no respect was the best in the remote yesterday more at fault than in its neglect of the sick and the handicapped. For centuries the church showed little sympathy or sense of responsibility for the sick and the handicapped. It maintained few or no hospitals, did little for sufferers from leprosy, cared not for the blind or the crippled, and made little effort to remove the causes of hunger, disease, and poverty. But when the church began to recover its integrity by a return to missionary obedience it developed concern for every kind of work that Jesus had done. And in every such area of concern much progress has been made. Missionary obedience led to the opening of hospitals abroad and that in turn stimulated the opening of hospitals at home. Sending missionaries to Africa awakened many Americans to the need for Christian attitudes toward their fellow citizens of African racial origin. Concern for sufferers from leprosy has led to the discovery of remedies that have now made it possible to free all mankind from this most prolific cause of misery. Christian missionaries have contributed powerfully to the conquest of many other scourges such as yellow fever, malaria, bubonic plague, cholera, yaws, sleeping sickness, and many forms of mental disturbance.

A program of missions suitable for this day's responsibilities would certainly call for a vast extension of medical service and its closest possible association with the total life of the church, in preaching, worship, and neighborhood service. Every Christian ought to be a soldier in the war against preventable disease and a witness to God's persistent love for all his children. In this world strategy the church in every nation should be called to full participation. Something is wrong whenever and wherever church members take only average interest in health and produce only their proportionate share of health workers. A civil surgeon in India, a government official responsible for supervising government hospitals in a large and populous area, remarked some years ago that Christians formed 1 per cent of the population in his district but provided 30 per cent of the staff in his hospitals and 3 per cent of the patients. His conclusion was that the church made people health conscious. He went farther and said, "Many Hindu and Moslem patients have been persuaded by Christian friends to come to the hospital for treatment."

Experience in modern missions teaches no lesson more clearly than that of the power that Christlike concern for needy people brings to evangelism. Everywhere people are learning that good religion helps to meet their felt needs and are abandoning past favorable attitudes toward religions that are indifferent to human need or seem to be powerless to help substantially. Asked why he had become a Christian a young African said: "When we were hungry after elephants had destroyed our fields, and lions had killed our cows, the Christians helped us. When we were sick and did not know how to get well the Christians opened a hospital for us. When we were illiterate the same people started a school in our village. And when some of my kind of people became Christians I saw that they took more interest in their neighbors. So I learned that the Christian religion is good and I accepted it."

An Aymara in Bolivia remarked, "My people have been mistreated a long time. I thought we had no friends. But the Evangelicals came teaching that God loves us as much as he does anybody on earth, and that they love us. I watched them and knew that they do love the poor and sick, so I believed their religion. And now I am an Evangelical and know God's love.

And my family knows that love has come into my heart and that I am changed. Now they, too, are becoming Evangelical Christians."

Love and sympathy must flow from the heart that Christ rules. How could it be otherwise when they flowed without ceasing from his heart when he was in the flesh? "If God so loved us, we also ought to love one another." "The wisdom from above is first pure, then peaceable, gentle, open to reason, full of mercy and good fruits, without uncertainty or insincerity." When Christians show love for needy and sinful men, making every effort to help them, they give powerful witness to Christ. Surely the great need today is not to return to the prevailing mediocrity of the past but to go forward to higher levels of faith and devotion. There is abundant reason to believe that the best days of the church lie ahead.

The church in many lands is incomparably stronger now than it was a generation ago. In India, for example, far more people are being taught everything that Jesus commanded his disciples. Well-trained Indian ministers have replaced missionaries from other lands, and while their numbers are by no means adequate for the task, they are able to serve the church much better than did their predecessors of any earlier period. Mighty Protestant churches have arisen in Brazil and Chile. African Christians are rapidly developing strength as they accept and meet obligations that were kept from them unwisely and unfairly until recently. The Chinese of the Dispersion numbering over twenty million are responsive to the Gospel as comparable numbers never were in mainland China. And many Chinese Christians are proving their faith despite the opposition of the Communist oppressors. Tremendous opportunity for the strengthening and

105

expansion of the church exists in nearly every part of today's world.

In these conditions, to realize its optimum growth and to make its maximum contribution to God and man, the church needs to move forward to that life and character for which it was made and to which it has ever been called.

VII

Potential Christian Nations of Tomorrow

The use of the term "Christian" in this chapter title is open to a number of objections. It cannot be exactly defined. There is no indication that Jesus ever called anybody a Christian or that while he was on earth in the flesh he ever heard anyone so called. He himself was acclaimed the Christ, but his disciples never called themselves Christians while he was with them in the flesh. That most honorable title was first used at Antioch, a tribute to disciples in recognition of the change that had been wrought in them. Paul and Barnabas had met with the church there for a whole year, teaching a growing brotherhood of disciples. Rapid growth had evoked this tribute. It is doubtful if the name Christian would ever have been given in a slow-growth situation. But here were multitudes passing from a state of sin known to all, through acceptance of Christ and active church membership, to a state of grace that all recognized.

When once the title was given, its use spread rapidly. Peter, in his first epistle, uses the expression in much the way it is used now the world over: "If one suffers as a Christian, let him not be ashamed, but under that name let him glorify God." And King Agrippa proved himself well acquainted with the use and meaning of the word, when at the trial of Paul he said, "In a short time you think to make me a Christian!" The king was declaring his surprise at the audacity of the prisoner for trying to make him a convert. Paul in reply by implication approved the word Christian and agreed that the king correctly understood his endeavor. "Whether short or long, I would to God that not only you but also all who hear me this day might become such as I am [a Christian]—except for these chains."

Paul never desired slow growth. When response was not forthcoming, he moved on to another place and continued persuading men that Jesus was the Savior. He was not with the eleven on the mountain in Galilee to hear the original proclamation of the Great Commission: "Go therefore and make disciples of all nations, baptizing them in the name of the Father and of the Son and of the Holy Spirit, teaching them to observe all that I have commanded you." But he accepted the commission fully and in every way consistent with his faith tried to make disciples of nations. He did not shy away from the rapid discipling of large groups. But then he had never heard of rugged individualism!

Whether any nation is worthy to be called Christian is beside the point. Perhaps few individuals are. But the great commission was not to make nations Christians but to make them disciples. And how Christian in fact were the eleven? They had failed, denied, and forsaken him. Probably none would have called himself or any of his fellows a Christian. All were, however, disciples. As disciples they could make disciples. In time they all became highly perfected Christians—wonderful, zealous, dedicated believers in and servants of Christ.

However strong the objections to the use of the term Christian may be, as applied to nations or to persons, it is too late now to rule it out. We will use it for nations where a majority of their citizens confess to believe in Christ and his teachings. In that sense, for example, Great Britain, Italy, the United States of America, Canada, and the Scandinavian nations, to name just a few, are Christian nations despite the presence of many unrepentant and continuing sinners in each of these countries. Sinners were in the church from the beginning, and there are many in every nation of disciples today. Paul made disciples in great numbers and encouraged them by calling them what they were only potentially—"saints"; though he recognized that they were far from being blameless. Their misconduct, of which he writes frankly, would make any church member of today ashamed. The world church is now far more Christian in character and behavior than was the church at Corinth that so troubled Paul.

Through modern missions a number of nations have been brought to Christian discipleship. Among them are various nations of Pacific Islanders. The ancient Hawaiians are now predominantly Christian in the faith they profess. The Fiji and Tonga islanders are united in discipleship. The Maoris of New Zealand are happily integrated with men of other racial origins as disciples. The Filipinos, with only small groups of the unconverted, are united in Christian belief. Roman Catholic missionaries fortunately reached the Philippines before the Moslems were able to extend their control to those islands as they had extended it to Java, and to some other parts of what is now Indonesia.

In nearby Sarawak, in the northwest corner of Borneo, a number of ancient races are undergoing radical change. Ahead of them is the possibility of being drawn into a common citizenship. One of the most interesting of those ancient nation-races or tribes is the Iban. They are often called "Dyaks" which means "wild men." They resent that name and call themselves "Ibans." They are a proud, handsome people who have been handicapped by a crude and cruel religion.

Into the fabric of that religion have been woven many ancient hatreds, a vast amount of superstition, bad social ethics, and erroneous thinking about agriculture. For many centuries they warred with other races and tribes. Fighting was continuous with never an interlude of peace. Young men were taught to kill members of the enemy tribes and to cut off and bring to their homes the heads of all whom they killed. Their religion told them that the strength of their enemies would by this means be transferred to them and to all who shared their longhouse abode.

In those conditions, community housing was necessary for defense. To live in an isolated home would have been an invitation to murder. So sites were chosen along the banks of the rivers, and houses were built on stilts or piles and reached by ladders which could be drawn up at night to prevent their use by attackers. These longhouses are not crude huts but solidly built structures, consisting of a front uncovered veranda, back of it a covered veranda and behind that the living quarters of the several families. This plan provides places for many types of work on and beneath the uncovered veranda. The covered veranda, which is often fifteen to twenty feet wide, runs the entire length of the longhouse which may be as much as a thousand feet or more. It provides for a full community life. On it children play their games, women gather in little groups, and men find recreation and entertainment, especially in cock-fighting. Nearly every family keeps two or more fighting cocks and at least one dog. Hanging in wicker baskets from the rafters of many longhouses are scores, and in some cases hundreds, of human skulls.

These Ibans are turning to Christ in large numbers. And the skulls are gradually disappearing, despite the strenuous objections of many of the older men and women. A young man told the writer, "When we worship the Eternal Father we are ashamed of our killing, and when we ask for the forgiveness of our sins we cannot be proud of the skulls." Under British rule the killings have been suppressed; and under Christian influence, which began through the witness of Chinese Christian merchants, faith in a better way of life has spread rapidly. An international missionary force is now reinforcing the testimony of the Chinese church. Welded together in a fellowship of love, Chinese, American, British, Filipino, Indian, and Indonesian missionaries are preaching, teaching, and confirming the gospel so effectively that the Ibans can unhesitantly be listed as a potential Christian nation of tomorrow. And the tribes with whom the Ibans have waged war across uncounted centuries are now calling for the gospel. A deputation from one of those tribes some time ago inquired, "Is the love you preach only for our former enemies or is it for us also? Please learn our language and preach to us!"

Ibans in one little area of Sarawak began confessing belief in Christ a hundred years ago, but the missionaries there had no idea of group action in religion and received very few converts. They were concerned to protect the church against the influx of illiterate people who came more rapidly than they

111

could be absorbed. A few families were raised in education, culture, health, and economic status but were thus separated from their people. The great mass of the Ibans was left untouched, except perhaps by a sense of loss and resentment. With the understandings that have come through the social sciences and experience of the church with closely integrated groups in many parts of the world, there can now be no excuse for detaching individual converts, subjecting them to the dangers of social dislocation, and destroying their potentialities for evangelism.

Fortunately the Ibans are now coming to Christian faith and purpose in large groups and there seems to be an excellent chance of bringing the nation as a whole to Christian discipleship. An adequate response by Christians to the call of the former enemies of the Ibans will bring those nations also into the fold of believers.

On the Asiatic mainland Korea is certainly a potential Christian nation of tomorrow. What has already been achieved since the first Protestant missionaries landed in Korea in 1885 makes one of the most encouraging stories in the history of the expansion of the church. Six missionaries representing two major American churches reached Korea together in the spring of 1885. They were soon reinforced by other missionaries from their respective churches. Other missions were opened later on, especially after the Second World War and the Korean War. During the rule of Japanese imperialism, the church was subject to much arbitrary interruption of its work. Nevertheless Christianity has become the most powerful religious force in the country. Syngman Rhee said several years ago while President that non-Christians as well as Christians in all branches of the

112

armed forces were demanding Christian chaplains. The National Museum, recently established and located on the former site of a Shinto temple, devotes more than half its space to exhibits representing the history of Christian missions and churches in Korea.

The churches have grown until they have more than a million members. In the capital city of Seoul alone these churches have over 250 congregations. A high proportion of Christians are tithers and members of Bible study classes. Early morning prayer meetings are held daily in many churches. In some evangelism is so emphasized that when new believers are enrolled and assigned to Bible study classes they are told that each of them must bring in at least one new believer before he or she can be baptized.

The leaders in nearly every aspect of national life are Christians. That is true in politics because in the struggle for freedom from exploitation of the masses by the old Korean dynasty and later in opposition to the tyranny of Japanese imperialism, Christians first helped to formulate and present the grievances of the common people. It is equally true in education, diplomacy, finance, and the defense services.

Christian preaching and teaching have produced a new national conscience. The Buddhist president of a government college, appealing for the appointment of a second Christian chaplain for his institution said: "There are over two thousand people connected with this college—students, staff, employees of all kinds, and the families of many of them—and no one chaplain can ever care adequately for that many people." Asked why he did not ask for a Buddhist chaplain when he and most of the students and employees and some of the staff were

113

Buddhists, he seemed shocked at the idea and replied, "As chaplain? What good could a Buddhist monk do? What would he know about God? (Buddhism is atheistic.) Only a Christian minister can help people solve moral and spiritual problems."

One cannot write about Korea as a potential Christian nation of tomorrow without a frank statement of two tragic developments which are now weakening the witness of the church and keeping thousands from acknowledging Christ as Lord and Savior.

The first is that much professional divisiveness has been imported from the United States and other nations. The Presbyterian Church of Korea has been split into four main bodies. The Methodist Church has also suffered but its divisions have hitherto been temporary or minor. So much energy has been expended in defending the church against imported strife that both the amount and the quality of evangelistic effort have declined.

The second is that many Christians in Korea, as in other countries in our own and earlier times, have failed to live as Christians should. Personal ambition has led to conflicts within the councils of the churches. Charges of corruption have been made by Christians against Christians. Old Testament thinking has at times been more apparent in the life of Christians and their teachings than the redemptive teachings of Jesus.

When we turn to Africa, we see a number of nations previously pagan which may within a few years turn to Christianity. They are definitely breaking with their past beliefs and practices in religion. For one hundred years they have been influenced by the Christian evangel and service. Large self-directive African churches have arisen. School systems have been

114

instituted and maintained. A vast program of medical relief has been carried on. Recently Islam and Communism have appeared on the scene and are making a considerable bid for the hearts of the pagan Africans.

In this triangular contest for the mind and heart of erstwhile pagan Africans, both Communism and Islam have certain advantages. Communism, coming just as these long-neglected children of God are comprehending in part the frightful cost of their past subservience to paganism, seems to them to speak the truth when it denounces religion as a harmful indulgence, serving the selfish desires of a minority at great cost to the nation. When the Communist says that white Christians have mistreated black Africans—taking vast numbers of them away into slavery, seizing land for their own purposes, expropriating mineral wealth, employing native Africans as servants for the hardest and least rewarding jobs while making fortunes for themselves and for those of their own people who are already living in luxury in far-off countries—it all seems reasonable to them. When they are told that no Communist nation has ever seized any African territory or carried away any African into slavery or removed from the reach of Africans any of the vast wealth of the continent, these Africans seem compelled to agree, "Yes, that is true." Then the Communist says, "The only white man you can trust is the white Communist," and he scores heavily.

Likewise Islam can score heavily in this contest. It appears among the common people in a friendly guise, free from barriers of race and color. The missionary of Islam is usually a nonprofessional. He comes as a trader or a government official. He is eager to spread his faith. He mingles with people freely and never stands aloof. To the African, Islam looks black and

115

that to him seems as important as keeping the congregation white seems to a member of the White Citizens Council in the deep South of the United States or to a devotee of apartheid in the Union of South Africa. More than that, the rich and the poor seem to the onlooking African closer together in Islam than in Christianity. At mosque worship, Moslems kneel in unsegregated rows and bow their heads to the floor in Islamic gestures of humble and united submission to Allah, while Christians tend to divide in worship services and church activity in accord with social and economic status.

It will surprise some Christians to read that Islam sometimes presents a kinder face than does Christianity. The Christian missionary's tendency to insist that men with more than one wife should keep only one and send others away as a condition of baptism or admission to Christian fellowship has imposed real hardships on many African women, respectably married, "who have been put aside by their husbands and deprived of their children." That action (compelling the breakup of families and the disavowal of marital obligations entered into according to the accepted code in pagan society) is seriously questioned today. It deprives a mother of her children and children of their mother's care. In any society that means extreme hardship both ways. It seems to be of the nature of committing sin so that grace may abound. (The theoretical possibility of the children going with the mother when she is discarded is said to be impractical at this time in Africa, because the father will not even consider letting any of his children leave.) How serious a situation results when wives are sent away is shown by the fact that many of them become prostitutes. Very often a good husband who eagerly desires to be accepted as a Christian feels he cannot

116

conscientiously renounce his obligations to the wives whom he is told to disown and send them away. Experience proves that many families kept out of the church over this issue have become determined defenders of polygamy and opponents of the church.

There is considerable evidence that the apostolic church received the polygamist and his wives into membership without demanding the dissolution of marriages consummated prior to conversion, but allowed no additional marriage for such a convert during the lifetime of his wives and strictly enforced monogamy for all others. Polygamy did not continue in the early church except in isolated cases, but the policies most commonly favored by church and mission today have not solved the problem in Africa. A solution is becoming very urgent now.

A British mission board executive, Cecil Northcott, has written that Islam's easygoing attitudes to polygamy are contrasted with Christianity's insistence on monogamy to the detriment of Christianity. The same author also contrasts Christianity as an individualistic religion to which you make your response and go your way with Islam as emphasizing brotherhood and togetherness which create a satisfying sense of belonging.

Something new in Islamic propaganda in Africa is the opening of a medical mission. This is done by a nontypical "modernist" sect of Islam known as Ahmadiyas. It originated in India but is now strongest in Pakistan. While Moslem masses in Arabia, Egypt, Afghanistan, and other Moslem lands live without even the simplest medical service, the Ahmadiyas are building and staffing a hospital to provide a ministry of medicine and surgery to pagan tribes in Sierra Leone. The Ahmadiyas declare a threefold purpose: (a) to reform and purge Islam, (b) to express Islam in a way understood in the modern world, and (c) to

117

answer the challenge of Christianity by copying and borrowing from Christian faith and practice.

While there is danger for Christians in easygoing optimism that ignores the opposition, there is greater danger in over-estimating it and underestimating what Christ and his church have done, are doing, and can do in Africa. In almost all countries of the once-dark continent the light of the gospel shines brightly now. There is a church rooted in local life and culture in nearly every tribal area. In some countries the church is still weak but in others it wields real power. Missionaries from abroad no longer direct the church, but they are welcomed as colleagues. They can do much better work because their national associates are now in charge. By exercising anything like their maximum potentials the indigenous churches and their missionary brothers and sisters can win against both Communism and Islam.

Despite the offense being given to the conscience of the whole church by the present government of the Union of South Africa, the profession of Christian faith by a majority of the people of that country makes us classify it as a Christian nation. Will it be Christian tomorrow? Who can say? The writer believes the Union will not only continue Christian but its remaining non-Christians will become Christians. To whom else will they go? Furthermore it will adopt a racial policy consistent with its professed faith. The ruling party in the Union is supported by many who in their private lives and personal contacts with nonwhite people show themselves disciples of Jesus Christ. A minister of the Dutch Reformed Church of the Union of South Africa, while visiting in America, said to the writer: "As long as I was in my homeland I thought my government was right. Now I know its policies are wrong—theologically, morally, and politically. What is damaging to the church elsewhere cannot be good for the church in South Africa. We have been blinded by misconceived self-interest."

In North and South Rhodesia and Nyasaland large African denominations of scores of thousands and in two cases of hundreds of thousands of members have arisen in the last sixty years. Rapid and sound church growth has marked these lands. The churches conduct a network of schools so that an educated African leadership seems guaranteed. Much yet remains to be done, of course. The churches continue to propagate their faith and the pagan reservoir grows smaller every year.

Politically the situation is uncertain. The federation of these three lands may continue or break up. But the church is accustomed to perilous times. It sails fast in foul weather. It will continue to grow in these East African countries. Consequently they may reasonably be listed as potential Christian nations of tomorrow. Islam is not an immediate threat to them, nor is Communism. The situation presents no reason for complacency nevertheless; apart from the complex of resentments over unmet political aspirations and racial discrimination, the church knows no handicaps other than such as emerge normally from man's proneness to sin and error.

Two normal handicaps, however, must be removed if the discipling of the nation is not to be needlessly delayed. First the tendency to denominational division must be curbed. Umtali and Salisbury have a disgraceful multiplicity of denominations and the disgrace belongs more to missionary organizations operating from other lands than to indigenous Christians. The other removable handicap is the excessive individualism that has fastened itself like a parasite upon the life of the church. Group

119

conversions are rare in these tribal countries! They should be the normal way of accepting the Christian faith.

In Kenya, Tanganyika, and Uganda the church seems to be in a healthy state. Adjustments in racial attitudes have proceeded rapidly in Kenya since the Mau Mau crisis. Christians have drawn together across the borders of race and tribe, and progress has been made in developing a consciousness of a multiracial and multilingual family of God. European Christians have been moved by the stalwart heroism of their African cobelievers who died for their faith in large numbers at the hands of fanatical fellow countrymen who gave them the choice of joining in murder or being murdered. Even the murderers were moved to admire the martyrs. The church in Kenya is growing now at an accelerated rate that seems likely to continue.

In Tanganyika a great Lutheran church of 300,000 members has arisen and is discipling the tribes. Numerous other churches and missions are encountering increasing responsiveness to the gospel. Multitudes as in the days of the New Testament church are being "added to the Lord." Race relations in Tanganyika during this generation have been better than in some other areas in Africa and are not now a serious deterrent to church growth.

In Uganda the church is less divided than in most countries and is close to having the support of a majority of the populace. National leadership in every sphere is largely Christian.

In all these countries in view of the extremely favorable circumstances, greater concern for more rapid growth of the church is urgently needed. The writer cannot suggest the rate of growth which may properly be sought, but it is sure that the growth rate of recent years—though good—can be and should be considerably augmented. Unless used now, the very favorable conditions may be lost.

In West Africa Protestant missions have served nobly for more than a hundred years. During the first two generations climate and disease took a heavy toll of missionaries. Liberia and Sierra Leone provided homes for liberated slaves, and have borne powerful witness to Christian opposition to that most vicious evil—slavery. Christians in Sierra Leone are said to number only 5 per cent of the population but their position in national life is strong. In view of the fact that a much larger percentage holds Christian ideals of behavior and religious beliefs, extended and intensified evangelism is overdue. Whole tribes should be claimed for Christ and confronted with the opportunity to decide for him in social units.

Liberia has a much larger proportion of Christians than Sierra Leone and they are a privileged group. They run the government, schools, public services, and to a considerable extent the economy. For a long time they neglected the pagan people of the interior. For the past two decades, however, there has been developing a commendable concern for neglected elements of the population. To make the most of present opportunities the church in Liberia, aided by its missionary societies, needs vigorously to expand preaching, teaching, and proving Christ's message of God's love and redemptive grace for sinful people everywhere. The church in Liberia and its assisting missions should take the discipling of its tribes with renewed seriousness.

The church in Ghana is strongly entrenched along the coast and in Ashanti. In the interior, the Northern Territories, are many pagans. They can be reached today but cannot be neglected with impunity. Fortunately Christians in and around Accra and in other well-developed areas are manifesting a growing interest in the evangelization of the interior tribes. The Northern Territories need many more missionaries—African, American, and European—soon. If they get them, Ghana too will become a Christian nation tomorrow.

In Nigeria Christians are in a majority in coastal areas, Moslems in the North, and pagans in between. The head of the government is an able Moslem. Pagans hold the balance of power. The Moslems are concerned about making converts but a recent observer estimates that the Nigerian churches still have an even chance to win these pagan peoples. To do so they must multiply their own missionary effort manyfold and recruit many more assistants abroad and set them to work. The battle to win status for national churchmen vis-à-vis the missionary has now been won. Nigerian churches must now learn how to use large numbers of missionaries from Asia as well as from the West to disciple remaining pagan populations.

Angola and Mozambique, huge African territories with immense resources, are ruled by Portugal under an absolute dictatorship. The people as a whole have no voice in their government, but that fact is camouflaged by Portuguese boasting of the alleged advantages of their assimilado policy which confers limited rights upon such Africans as learn to speak, read, and write Portuguese, and are accepted by Portuguese officials as worthy of citizenship. People of Portuguese origin and those whom the Portuguese have certified as assimilated obtain many advantages in education, government employment, and business opportunities. Others are heavily taxed and restricted. The Roman Catholic Church is favored, and Protestant Christians

122

are generally suspected of being at least unenthusiastic about Portuguese rule. Seventeen African ministers of one Protestant church have been murdered by Portuguese military forces and civilian settlers during this year, and tens of thousands of Protestant and pagan people have been slaughtered. As this is written thousands are in jail.

Thus in these two countries, there exist side by side large vigorous Protestant churches and a religious vacuum. The Roman Catholic Church, allied with the foreign tyranny, is heavily handicapped. As these countries become self-governing, the turn to Protestant Christianity will be marked. It may be tremendous.

If the Portuguese were asked whether Angola and Mozambique should be counted as potential Christian nations of tomorrow, they would answer that both nations are Christian now and will be Christian tomorrow, and by Christian they would mean Roman Catholic. They insist that neither country is a colony, but that both are districts of Portugal. In the Africa of a short time hence Angola and Mozambique will be independent nations and the European empires only a bad memory. In that day both nations will probably be Christian.

Congo too will most likely be one of the active and powerful Christian nations of tomorrow. Christward movements of large dimensions and power have developed within many Congolese tribes. All the characteristics of the New Testament church are found in Congo churches. In revival meetings thousands come from all directions, African ministers call to penitence and faith, and men and women confess their sins and pray fervently for forgiveness. Islam can nowhere match that for emotional appeal nor produce such moral transformation or personality enrich-

123

ment as abound where these revivals have taken place. Multitudes continue to be added to the Lord in Congo.

Until its closing years, the late Belgian government limited educational opportunity severely. That fact has handicapped the churches, depriving them of educated ministerial and lay leaders. Now a crash program to provide better educated Congolese leadership for men and women whose training was interrupted promises large results. And high schools, colleges, and a technological institute are planned. These greatly reinforce the prospects of Congo becoming a Christian nation.

While the ultimate decisions that will determine the actual future in all of these potential Christian nations will be made by the citizens of these nations, no reader of this book, and no member of the church of Christ anywhere is without a measure of responsibility for influencing these decisions. The kind of Christians we are wherever we live in this changing world, and the degree of our obedience to our Lord's command to disciple the nations will make a difference in each of these countries.